STORMIE OMARTIAN

JUST ENOUGH LIGHT

for the STEP

I'M ON

Trusting God in the Tough Times

HARVEST HOUSE PUBLISHERS

EUGENE, OREGON

Cover by Koechel Peterson & Associates, Minneapolis, Minnesota

Photograph on p. 10 by Patrick Raffy Frantz, Patrick Frantz Photography, Granada Hills, CA. Used by permission.

Cover photo © photos.com

JUST ENOUGH LIGHT FOR THE STEP I'M On
Copyright © 1999/2008 by Stormie Omartian
Published by Harvest House Publishers
Eugene, Oregon 97402
www.harvesthousepublishers.com

Library of Congress Cataloging-in-Publication Data

Omartian, Stormie.
    Just enough light for the step I'm on / Stormie Omartian.
        p. cm.
    ISBN 978-0-7369-2357-6

    1. Trust in God—Christianity. I. Title
BV4637.O44 1999
242—dc21   98-42889
        CIP

Printed in the United States of America

11   12   13   / VP /   10   9

Acknowledgments

With special thanks:

- ✿ to my husband, Michael, for believing so strongly in me and in this book.

- ✿ to my children, Mandy, Chris, and John, for your love and support.

- ✿ to my prayer partners and dear friends, Susan Martinez, Katie Stewart, Donna Summer Sudano, Roz Thompson, and Jan Williamson, for your prayers and encouragement.

- ✿ to my wonderful secretary, sister, and friend, Susan Martinez, for blessing my life in so many ways.

- ✿ to Bob Hawkins, Jr., Carolyn McCready, Bill Jensen, Julie Tingstrom, Teresa Evenson, Ruth Samsel, Barb Sherrill, Janna Walkup, and Betty Fletcher for catching the vision for this book and making it all happen. You are the best!

- ✿ to Patrick Raffy Frantz for your inspiring photographs, my favorite of which appears in the beginning of this book.

Contents

Introduction

ore and more, God is teaching me to trust Him for every step I take. He constantly calls me to stretch beyond what's comfortable. To walk through new territory when I would rather stay with the familiar. To face difficult physical, mental, and emotional challenges. To do things I know I can't achieve by myself without His power. Each time something is required of me that I'm certain I am unable to accomplish in my own strength, I see a picture of just one or two steps being illuminated, while those before and after are engulfed in darkness and cannot be seen. This describes my walk with God. I trust Him for each day of life, grateful for every breath, determined to look for the blessing in the moment, no matter what the circumstances. I follow His lead—even when I can't see where I'm going, even when it scares me to do so—because deep within my spirit I know that these simple steps of faith are preparing me for eternity.

—Stormie Omartian

... come and let us walk in
the light of the LORD.

Isaiah 2:5

Just Enough Light

Sometimes only the step I'm on,
   or the very next one ahead,
      is all that is illuminated for me.
God gives just the amount of light I need
   for the exact moment I need it.
At those times I walk in surrender to faith,
   unable to see the future
   and not fully comprehending the past.
And because it is God who has given me
   what light I have,
      I know I must reject the fear and
      doubt that threaten to overtake me.
I must determine to be content where
   I am, and allow God to get me where I
      need to go.
I walk forward,
     one step at a time,
       fully trusting that
         the light God sheds
           is absolutely sufficient.

Life is a walk.
Each day we take
steps. Our tomorrow
is determined by
the steps we
take today.

ONE

Learning to Walk

Life is a walk. Each day we take steps. Our tomorrow is determined by the steps we take today.

When both of my children learned to walk, they didn't get very far without falling. They fared much better if they reached up and took my hand. Or their father's hand. We were able to guide them away from danger and get them safely where they needed to go. But sometimes they quickly headed off without our help. My son would end up falling down and hurting himself, or my daughter would wander off to someplace she wasn't supposed to go and get into trouble. Occasionally we *allowed* those things to happen because we wanted them to eventually learn to walk *without* our assistance. Of course, we did step in and protect them when we saw danger. But our goal was always to prepare them for the day when they would no longer need our help. And we were thrilled when we saw them experience that joy of freedom for the first time.

Learning to walk with our Heavenly Father is somewhat different. He wants us to reach up and take His hand, but He doesn't want us to *ever* let go. In fact, His desire is that we become *more* and *more* dependent upon Him for every step. That's because He wants to take us to places we've never been. To heights we can't even imagine. In order to do that, we have to go through the low valleys, treacherous mountains, rough terrain, and narrow paths of life—places where we could easily get lost or off the track. And there is definitely no way we can just head off on our own and expect to arrive safely in the place He has planned for us. And, quite opposite of the way we teach our children, we will *never* know the joy of *true* freedom until we understand we cannot take a single step without His help.

But it's up to us to take the first step. If we don't, we will never learn to walk with Him. We can be so afraid of taking a wrong step that we fail to take any step at all. God didn't part the waters of the Jordan River for the Israelites until they first put their feet in the water (Joshua 3:15-16). That's because God always requires the first step to be ours. In order to take that first step, we must look into the face of God, reach up to take His hand, and say, "Lead me in the path You have for me, Lord. From this day on I want to walk with You. I take this step of faith and I trust You to meet me here. Align my heart with Yours."

Once you've taken *that* first step, God will show you other steps to take. He will teach you how to walk in the light of His truth, revelation, and love. You'll discover ways to avoid the things that separate you from Him and all He has for you. You'll learn to walk away from fear, depression, condemnation, loneliness, loss, unforgiveness, and disappointment. You'll understand what it means to walk through the dark times of your life with the comfort of His presence as your only light.

I know what it's like to walk without His light. In my teens and twenties, I wandered around in a confusion of drugs, alcohol, occult practices, eastern religions, and unhealthy relationships, trying to find an escape from the emotional pain I endured daily. I was desperately struggling to live, but was moving closer to death with every decision I made and step I took. I experienced it all, but nothing worked and I became desperate. As I carefully planned my suicide, I knew I didn't really want to die. But I couldn't live with the pain anymore, and I had no other way to stop it.

When a close friend saw my hopelessness and took me to meet her pastor, I found what I had been searching for all along. Pastor Jack Hayford showed me that I had been crying out for love, acceptance, purpose, fulfillment, peace, and joy, and that these things could only be found in one place. When I prayed, "Jesus, come into my heart. Forgive me for not living Your way and lead me on the path You have for me," I knew I had found that place. It was at His feet. I felt hope for the very first time. It was the initial and pivotal step on a journey that would transform my life.

No matter how far away from God you've gone, when you surrender your life to the Lord, a path is carved from where you are to where you are supposed to be, and He puts you on it.

This is the miracle of His power. If the path you've been on is crooked, He will make it straight. If you are headed in the wrong direction, He will turn you around. If you have come to a standstill, He will get you moving. If you are going around in circles, He will correct your course and cause you to arrive at your destination. The simple act of giving your

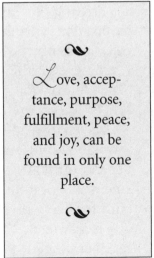

∽

*L*ove, acceptance, purpose, fulfillment, peace, and joy, can be found in only one place.

∽

life to Him will immediately put you on the correct path and aim you in the right direction.

As you take one step at a time, holding God's hand and letting Him lead, He will get you where you need to go.

The moment I made that decision, I felt a major course-correction happen. I didn't know where I was headed, but I saw a light at the end of the long, dark tunnel of my life and I started going toward it, away from the life I had known. Away from the ungodly friends, the destructive habits, the self-promotion. Away from hopelessness, depression, and futility. The road was not smooth and I fell a number of times, not because God let go of me, but because I let go of Him. But every time I reached out for His hand, He was always there to help me get back up and on the path again.

I have now been walking with the Lord for nearly thirty years. When I look back, I see that I was a different person then and living a whole other life. I know that I would never want to return to the way things were. Yet I occasionally find myself reverting to the old habit of trying to do things my own way. I sometimes forget that I need to depend on Him for every step.

Pastor Jack told me a story of a man who prayed, "Lord, I haven't done anything wrong today. I have not made any mistakes, spoken any wrong words, or thought any bad thoughts. I've done everything right so far. But I'm really going to be depending on You now, Lord, because I'm about to get out of bed."

Haven't we all felt like that sometimes? But that's the way God wants us to feel. He doesn't want us to just depend on Him as a last resort when we have a medical emergency or a financial crisis. He wants us to depend on Him for every breath we take. And, quite opposite of the way it may seem, that kind of dependent life is not stifling. It's liberating!

Learning to walk with God is a process. And just when we think we have it all figured out, God leads us into a new place where our old tricks won't work. In fact, it may seem like we're learning how to walk all over again. And in a way we are. We enter unfamiliar territory and are soon reminded that, on our own, we stumble. Yet when we take His hand, we fly. God wants us to soar far above the limitations of our lives and ourselves. He wants to take us to a place we have never been before and can't get to from where we are without His help.

When God used Moses to lead the Israelites out of Egypt, they had to learn to depend on the Lord for every step of their journey to the Promised Land. When they did not do that, they got into trouble. It's the same for us today. God moves us out on a path to someplace we've never been before, and we believe we're failing if we have to depend on Him to get there. We try to make it on our own because we think that dependency is a sign of weakness, instead of understanding that it signals our willingness to allow God to be strong in us.

If you are at a place in your life where you feel like you can't take one step without the Lord's help, be glad. He has you where He wants you. If you're wondering, "Have I done something wrong?" the answer is most likely, "No, you've done something right." God has you on this path, no matter how difficult and impossible it may seem right now, because you are willing to follow Him. He wants to accomplish great things through you that can only come out of a life of faith. He wants your undivided attention because you can't do these

✺

*G*od moves us out on a path to someplace we've never been before, and we believe we're failing if we have to depend on Him to get there.

✺

things on your own. The path is not a punishment; it's a privilege. It's not a restriction; it's a reward.

God loves us so much that He allows us to get into difficult places in our lives so we will realize how dependent upon Him we must be.

If you have been walking with God for some time and you suddenly feel like your life has come to a halt, don't be alarmed. Most likely, God is adjusting your way. Having God correct your course doesn't necessarily mean the one you were on was incorrect. But it does mean that something needs to change to get you headed in the direction God wants to take you. And it doesn't matter how young or old you are. As long as you are breathing, God will have new paths for you to take and exciting things for you to do. It's best to trust His leading and get on with it. This is what a walk of faith is all about.

Abraham was walking by faith when God led him out of all that was familiar to him to a place he had never been. He knew God had called him from where he was, but he didn't know where God was leading. And Abraham's is one of the greatest stories in the Bible in regard to walking in faith: ". . . he went out, not knowing where he was going" (Hebrews 11:8).

How often have we felt like that? We go out because God is leading us, but we don't really know where we're headed.

Pastor Jack Hayford says, "It's a more certain proposition to follow the Lord, not knowing where you're going, than to think you know where you're going and you're not following the Lord."[1]

How true!

You might want to read the above quote several more times. It will be a great comfort to you on those days when you wonder if you're actually going *anywhere*. Don't worry, we've all had them. Abraham had them. Moses had them. Noah had them. All great godly people in history have had them. God doesn't often reveal the details of where He's taking you because He wants you to trust Him for every step. He wants you to pray and listen to Him directing your path for this day, this week, this season, this year, and this time.

When you hear God telling you to move in a certain direction, let me give you two words of advice: *Do it!* Refusing to walk according to God's leading will get you nowhere. Oh, you will arrive someplace all right, but if it is not where God wants to bless you, it will still be nowhere.

It doesn't matter what your situation is at this moment. Wherever you are, God has a path for you that is filled with good things. Draw close to Him and you'll find it. Say, "Show me the way in which I should walk and the thing I should do" (Jeremiah 42:3). He will do that and, if you carefully follow as He guides you, He will not let you get off the path. With each step He will reveal more of Himself. "Your ears shall hear a word behind you, saying, 'This is the way, walk in it'" (Isaiah 30:21). So reach up right now and take God's hand. He promises He won't let you fall.

Prayer Light

*F*ather God, I don't want to take one step without You. I reach up for Your hand and ask that You lead me in Your way. Thank You that no matter where I am right now, even if I have gotten way off course, in this moment as I put my hand in Yours, You will make a path from where I am to where I need to be. And You will lead me on it. I love that Your grace abounds to me in that way. Keep me on the path You have for me and take me where You want me to go. "Cause me to know the way in which I should walk, for I lift up my soul to You" (Psalm 143:8). I know that when I try to run the race without You, I get off course. So I commit this day to walk Your way. Thank You that even if I become weak and stumble, You will help me to rise again and continue on. And though I can't see exactly where I am going, I'm certain that *You* can and will enable me to get to where I need to be. Thank You, Lord, that You are teaching me how to walk in total dependence upon You, for I know therein lies my greatest blessing.

Footlights

O LORD, I know the way of man
is not in himself; it is not in man who
walks to direct his own steps.

JEREMIAH 10:23

You will show me the path of life;
In Your presence is fullness of joy;
At Your right hand are pleasures forevermore.

PSALM 16:11

A man's heart plans his way,
But the LORD directs his steps.

PROVERBS 16:9

The steps of a good man are
ordered by the LORD,
And He delights in his way.

PSALM 37:23

Come, and let us go up to the mountain of the LORD,
To the house of the God of Jacob;
He will teach us His ways,
And we shall walk in His paths.

MICAH 4:2

TWO

Beginning to See the Light

Our lives are touched by many different kinds of light.

Sunlight and moonlight. Stoplights and spotlights. Fire-light, city lights, candlelight, and lamplight. Headlights, night-lights, neon lights, and streetlights. Glittering and blinding lights. Confusing and deceiving lights.

All of these lights have one thing in common. They eventually go out. They're not reliable. They can never be the light we need to illuminate the path of our life. There is only one light that never goes out. It comes from God.

It *is* God.

God's light is the true light. His light makes clear. All other light confuses. His light *reveals* the truth. All other light obscures it. His light brings us out of our blindness, and helps us see in a way we've never been able to see before. He says, "I will bring the blind by a way they did not know; I will lead them in paths they have not known. I will make darkness light before them, and crooked places straight. These things I will do for them, and not forsake them" (Isaiah 42:16). God's light penetrates darkness, and darkness cannot put it out.

Unless we follow the true light, we are being led into darkness.

In the years before I had a personal relationship with God, I walked in a thick darkness of depression, fear, anxiety, and despair. Everything I experimented with was a desperate search for something to light up my life. But I never found anything lasting. When I received the Lord I was not suddenly flooded with light, as some people have described it. The light I saw was a glimmer of hope. I compare it to sleeping in a dark room with a pinhole of light entering through the curtain and shining brightly in your eyes. It's a small light, but noticeably bright enough to awaken you if you've grown accustomed to the blackness of the room. The light of the Lord was that unmistakable to me because of the contrasting darkness of my life. Any more light would have been blinding. But because of my own bondage, the light was dim at the beginning of my walk compared to what was to come.

From that day on, I walked toward the light. There were times when I took a wrong turn and fell into sudden darkness, but I found it so shocking and repulsive that I quickly got back on track. The more I walked in the light of the Lord, the brighter it became until it lit up every part of my being.

I have heard people talk about near-death experiences where they saw a bright light. I don't doubt that they saw it. But I know that when we who believe in the Lord die, we won't see *a* light. We will see *the* light. We will see Jesus who is the light of the world. The best way to make sure we see His light after we die is to follow His light as long as we're alive.

We begin to see the light when we begin to see the Lord.

The way to keep from following the wrong light is to not follow any light except for the light of Jesus. The world wants us to follow *its* light. The devil wants us to follow *his* light. "For Satan himself transforms himself into an angel of light" (2 Corinthians 11:14). We will encounter people who fancy themselves to be our savior and will want us to follow *their* light. But God does not have us follow a light. He has us follow *Him*. And He becomes our light. The more faithfully we follow Him, the more of His light we will have shining on our path. "In Him was life, and the life was the light of men" (John 1:4).

God's light is constant because *He* is constant. He is without change. His light doesn't grow dim or go out. If it appears to, it's because we have stepped out of the light of His presence. Although God is omnipresent, we must remember that there are degrees of the fullness of His presence we can enjoy and experience. He gives us as much of His presence as we are able to receive. Although His light never goes out, we sometimes do things that separate us from the fullness of His life and cause His light to appear dim in our lives.

King David was a man who went through some very dark times. Some of them were his fault (his immoral relationship with Bathsheba), and some of them weren't (his volatile relationship with the jealous King Saul). In either case, David always knew that the light on his path came from God. He was still God's anointed no matter how dark it got. Even when he made bad choices, he had a heart for the Lord. And God never allowed him to be destroyed.

It's the same with those of us who love God. His light is always

🙞

*G*od does not have us follow a light. He has us follow *Him*. And *He* becomes our light.

🙞

available to us. No matter how badly we think we've blown it in our lives, we are never truly in darkness when we look to Him.

Our problem is that when we enter into a dark time, we don't always realize that we have a light within us which never goes out. Jesus said, "I am the light of the world. He who follows Me shall not walk in darkness, but have the light of life" (John 8:12). If we don't understand what that verse means, we can get confused and begin to doubt. We see darkness and run after a light that is unreliable, instead of opening our eyes to follow the true light that cannot be extinguished.

During my first year as a new believer, every time anything went wrong I thought God had abandoned me. I felt like I was moving backward. I didn't realize that the layers of darkness I had lived a lifetime with needed to be stripped away so I could be free of them. In order to do that, I should have turned to God each time they surfaced. Instead, when the darkness of depression descended upon me as it had so many times in the past, I thought God was not there for me and so I sought out the old familiar comforts of ungodly relationships and alcohol. I became sidetracked and wasted precious time. None of this would have happened if I had made a strong effort to walk in the light every day, no matter what was going on in my life.

I have electricity in my home, but if I don't plug into it, I don't see the light. I have Jesus in my heart, but if I don't plug into Him daily, I won't see His light either, even though it is there. I have to connect with Him. Talk to Him. Worship Him. Spend time with Him. Bask in His radiance

*N*o matter how badly we think we've blown it in our lives, we are never truly in darkness when we look to Him.

like bathing in the sun. Become so familiar with *His* illumination of my soul that I immediately recognize any counterfeit.

I remember a conversation I had with a man who works as a night watchman. He described how he always looked intensely for the first sign of morning light, because that meant he and the property he had been guarding were out of danger and he could be relieved from the burden. God wants us to look for *His* light in our lives even "more than those who watch for the morning" (Psalm 130:6). That means we don't rest until we know we see it.

Whenever we go through difficult times, we anticipate the coming moment when all the pressure is off, the worry has subsided, the healing has manifested, the sadness has lifted, and the pain is gone. We continuously look for God to take away the discomfort we are experiencing. But God wants us to know that even as we wait for those changes to happen, His light is there *all* the time shining into our darkness. He wants us to trust that, and open our eyes to see it.

No matter how dark things seem in your life, when you walk with God you will find an abundance of His light right where you are. You will never be without it because you have the source of true and everlasting light within you. "The city had no need of the sun or of the moon to shine in it, for the glory of God illuminated it. The Lamb is its light" (Revelation 21:23). When God is your light, you have no need of any other.

So don't worry about seeing or understanding what the future holds. God wants you to trust Him as He leads you, even though you can't see clearly ahead. And don't be overly concerned about fully comprehending the past. Only He knows the whole truth about it, anyway. You have *Him* now. *He* is your light. And that's all that matters.

———————— *Prayer Light* ————————

ord, You are the light of my life. You illuminate my path, and I will follow wherever You lead. Shield me from being lured by the light of the world. Keep me from being deceived by the light of evil. Protect me from being blinded by the light that confuses. Help me to always identify the counterfeit. I depend on You to lift up the light of Your countenance upon me (Psalm 4:6). Thank You, Lord, that because You never change, Your light is constant in my life no matter what is going on around me. Shine Your light through me as I walk with my hand in Yours. I give this day to You and trust that the light You give me is just the amount I need for the step I'm on.

Footlights

This is the message which we have heard
from Him and declare to you, that
God is light and in Him is
no darkness at all.

If we say that we have fellowship
with Him, and walk in darkness,
we lie and do not practice the truth.

But if we walk in the light as He is in the
light, we have fellowship with one another,
and the blood of Jesus Christ His Son
cleanses us from all sin.

1 JOHN 1:5-7

That was the true Light which gives light to
every man coming into the world.

JOHN 1:9

While you have the light, believe in the light,
that you may become sons of light.

JOHN 12:36

The path of the just is like the shining sun,
That shines ever brighter unto the perfect day.

PROVERBS 4:18

God is the LORD,
And He has given us light . . .

PSALM 118:27

THREE

Refusing to Be Afraid of the Dark

Darkness is the absence of light. Everything is dark until light is brought into it. If we don't have the true light, we live in darkness. If we have the light in us that cannot be extinguished, then we can never be in total darkness.

There are different kinds of darkness, however, and we need to be able to discern one from the other. There is spiritual darkness that happens when we refuse to let God enter into our lives. There is the darkness of negative emotions like ignorance, pride, jealousy, anger, or hatred. There is the darkness we experience when we make selfish demands that satisfy our flesh at the expense of others. There is the darkness of living in disobedience to God's ways.

All of these kinds of darkness come about because of our own choices. "Those who sat in darkness and in the shadow of death, bound in affliction and irons—because they rebelled against the words of God, and despised the counsel of the Most High . . ." (Psalm 107:10-11).

Yet as damaging as our mistakes can be, God gives us a way out of the darkness we get ourselves into. "Then they cried out to the LORD in their trouble, and He saved them out of their distresses. He brought them out of darkness and the shadow of death, and broke their chains in pieces" (Psalm 107:13-14). When we return to Him, He restores us to the full light. Even if we foolishly create our own darkness, as long as we have a personal relationship with the Lord, His light *in* us cannot be put out.

When I gave birth to my first baby, the doctor told me, "You have a boy." I didn't forget that information and have to keep asking him over and over "What was my baby?" I did not wake up in the hospital the next morning and say to the nurse, "Tell me again what I had." I didn't call my best friend the following week and wonder, "Do you happen to remember whether I gave birth to a boy or girl?" The minute I heard I had a son, no one had to tell me again. From that moment, I knew. An entire vision for my child's future was in place the second I was told the truth.

This experience is the same for every mother and every father. Or anyone who receives lifechanging good news.

God wants you to have that same certainty about Him. He wants you to be so convinced of His presence in your life that even when you can't feel it, sense it, or see it, you know He is there. He wants you to be completely sure that the light of His Spirit *in* you will never be put out. You don't have to keep looking for it. You don't have to doubt it. No circumstance can dim it. It is there for now and all eternity.

One of the ways God makes us certain of His light is by allowing us to test it in the darkness. But this darkness is not to be dreaded. It is

> ∾
>
> *God* wants you to be so convinced of His presence in your life that even when you can't feel it, sense it, or see it, you know He is there.
>
> ∾

the darkness God has created for His purposes. "I form the light and create darkness . . ." (Isaiah 45:7). God sometimes allows things to get very dark in our lives in order to grow us up and teach us about Himself. And some things that we accomplish in darkness cannot happen in any other setting.

Think about what it's like when the power goes out in your home at night. You can barely function in the dark. You walk carefully, one step at a time, reaching out for familiar things to steady and guide you until you can find a flashlight, candle, or generator switch. If someone is holding a source of light, you reach out and take their hand so you can move together. You don't take a step until you're certain that both of you are going in the same direction.

That's exactly how God uses darkness in our lives. We're in the dark until we see *His* light in it. He wants us to reach out for *Him* so we can walk together in the same direction. He desires that we draw close so that we sense His presence at all times.

This is not like the darkness of evil, which you can clearly sense. Or the darkness of our own disobedience, which we know in our hearts. This is a different kind of darkness, and God says there are treasures to be found there. "I will give you the treasures of darkness and hidden riches of secret places, that you may know that I, the LORD, who calls you by your name, am the God of Israel" (Isaiah 45:3).

The treasure we find in the darkness is Him.

I have gone through dark times with my children, my marriage, my health, my work, and my relationships, and for many years I didn't realize that God was using these situations to increase my knowledge of Him. Now that I look back, I realize these were the very times that I had the greatest sense of His presence in my life. The more serious the difficulty, the more fervently I reached out to Him. As a result, my perception of who God is grew deeper and deeper. I discovered the amazing largeness of His love and grace toward those who walk closely with Him. Some things we only learn in the dark.

I'm not saying that God causes bad things to happen in our lives. He doesn't. We live in a fallen world and bad things happen. But God works in the midst of even the deepest darkness. His presence and His light are there for those who open their eyes to see it, and He brings good out of every situation.

If God desires to teach us things about Himself that we will only learn in the dark—when we are walking closely with Him and He has our undivided attention—then we will be the losers if we resist Him or our circumstances during this time. He wants to share His secrets with us. "He reveals deep and secret things; He knows what is in the darkness, and light dwells with Him" (Daniel 2:22). The biggest mistake we can make during this dark time is to be angry with God because we are in it. "'Woe to him who strives with his Maker!'" (Isaiah 45:9).

When I was pregnant with my second child, I was extremely sick. Month after month I went in and out of the hospital, so ill with nausea and pain that I could barely function. I felt like I was dying and truly didn't know if I could carry my child to full term. During this very dark time, I couldn't understand why God didn't heal me or at least give me some sign of relief. Anyone who has walked through the dark night of physical suffering knows what I am talking about.

One morning in the midst of deep despair, I bitterly asked God what I had done to deserve this agony. At nearly that same moment I received a call from Pastor Jack wanting to know if my husband and I would become leaders in a new area of ministry at our church. It was a position that required great trust and—in view of my recent attitude of striving with my Maker—I felt especially unworthy. When I hung up the telephone, I was deeply repentant.

My experience taught me that even in the darkest times, we should never doubt God. Even when it may *appear* like our life is over and He has forgotten us, He is actually growing us into our future.

Sometimes what seems like the darkest step we've ever been on comes just before the brightest light we've ever experienced.

That's why we can't be angry about being in the dark. People who doubt God in the midst of darkness and blame Him for their discomfort don't really know Him. If they really knew Him, they would never feel that way.

Obviously I didn't know Him as well as I thought I did. But I came to know Him in a much deeper way through that experience. Eventually I was healed of my sickness, I gave birth to a healthy baby girl, doors of opportunity opened for my writing, and our family was blessed in countless ways. I am embarrassed to think that I had doubted God's goodness. In the darkness of the situation I had given up hope, and here He was about to do something great. I had doubted His light was there for me, but it had never changed because *He* will never change.

Often when we find ourselves in the midst of a dark situation, we immediately believe we must be out of the will of God. That might be true, but if we've been living in obedience to the Lord to the best of our ability, we are more likely right in the *center* of God's will. In fact, God's will can lead us into some very dark circumstances. Oswald Chambers

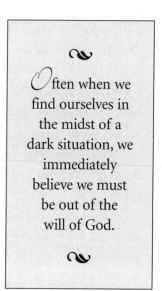

∾

*O*ften when we find ourselves in the midst of a dark situation, we immediately believe we must be out of the will of God.

∾

said, "Let it be understood that the darkness our Lord speaks of is not darkness caused by sin or disobedience, but rather darkness caused by excess light. . . . Such times of darkness come as a discipline to the character and as the means of fuller knowledge of the Lord." [1]

When we find ourself in the dark, we must *stop* what we're doing, *look* for His light, and *listen* for His voice. If He is directing us, yet we ignore it, fail to see it, refuse to do it, run from it, don't comprehend it, or deliberately disobey it, we will be miserably lost. We have to be still and know that He is God. We have to reach out to Him and He will give us a sense that He is there.

When my son was a small child, every evening I read a bedtime story to him, put him in his crib, and turned out the light. Then sometimes I would lie down on the floor beside his bed with a pillow under my head. It had a calming effect on both of us. We would occasionally sing little songs, but usually we simply lay quietly there together. Whenever I reached up my hand in the dark, his tiny hand always found mine and held on. It was one of those precious moments you like to remember when your children become teenagers.

I think it is even more precious to our Heavenly Father when we reach out in the dark and find *His* hand waiting for us. So many times I felt alone and afraid in the darkness of my circumstances, yet when I reached out to God I always found His presence there, calming, reassuring, protecting, and loving me. I know to expect it now. I am certain that even in my darkest times, when I can't see anything, God is there and will not forsake me. He wants us to trust Him so completely that He can take us on a journey where *His* light is our *only* light. Then when we take His hand, He can lead us anywhere.

The unknown can be frightening, but when we immerse ourselves in the presence of the Lord, we can know *Him* in it. His love takes away our fear. When we take a step, His light is with us. When we take the next step, His light is with us still. Sometimes we stumble around faithlessly in the dark and don't even recognize His light when we have it. I did that when I questioned God during my difficult pregnancy. I was walking in the light and thought I was in the dark. In the dark season of my own soul, I failed to see that His light had never left me. "The light shines in the darkness, and the darkness did not comprehend it" (John 1:5).

When we walk with the Lord, the dark is actually a place we can never fully be.

The unknown is not so frightening when we realize that our all-knowing God is in it. We know *Him*. And once we experience His light in the midst of darkness, our darkness will never be the same.

If you feel like you're in a dark place in your circumstances right now, know that God has not abandoned you. You are not wandering aimlessly. He sees the path you are on. "For the ways of man are before the eyes of the LORD, and He ponders all his paths" (Proverbs 5:21). He is there with you in great power and wants you to realize how much He loves you. If you're in darkness as a result of your own choices, confess that to Him and He will lead you out of it. If it is a darkness He has created to grow your faith, be joyful. There are awesome treasures of His presence ahead for you.

Don't be afraid of the dark. Instead of seeing the darkness as frightening, view it as a precious and wonderful place to be. When everything around you gets darker, the light inside you will grow brighter. God will speak to you and give you illumination right where you are. He wants you to reach up, take His hand, and walk every step with Him. He wants you to rest in the knowledge that the light He gives you, His light that is in you, is enough light to keep you securely on the path.

Prayer Light

*L*ord, thank You that because I walk with You I don't have to fear the dark. Even in the blackest night, You are there. In the darkest times, You have treasures for me. No matter what I am going through, Your presence and grace are my comfort and my light. Your Word says, ". . . if one walks in the night, he stumbles, because the light is not in him" (John 11:9-10). But I know Your light *is* in me. Jesus, You have come as a light into the world so that whoever believes in You should not abide in darkness (John 12:46). I believe in You and know that You have lifted me out of the darkness of hopelessness, futility, and fear. I refuse to be afraid. I confess any time I have chosen to walk in the darkness of doubt, disobedience, or blaming You for my circumstances. Forgive me. I give my hand to You, Lord. Take hold of it and lead me. Thank You that as I take each step, the light You give me will be all I need.

Footlights

Who walks in darkness and has no light?
Let him trust in the name of the Lord
And rely upon his God.

Isaiah 50:10

They need no lamp nor light of the sun,
for the Lord God gives them light.

Revelation 22:5

Even the night shall be light about me;
Indeed, the darkness shall not hide from You,
But the night shines as the day; The darkness and
the light are both alike to You.

Psalm 139:11-12

For You will light my lamp;
The Lord my God will enlighten my darkness.

Psalm 18:28

The people who sat in darkness have seen a
great light, and upon those who sat in the
region and shadow of death
light has dawned.

Matthew 4:16

FOUR

Embracing the Moment

None of us like pain, uncertainty, strife, or frustration. We want things to run along smoothly. But the challenging and miserable times are not without their aspect of good. Things happen to us during those times that are as precious as diamonds. For it is then that we have the opportunity to experience the Lord's presence in a deeper way. If we embrace the moment, we see Him in it.

The first winter after my family and I moved to Tennessee from sunny Southern California, we found ourselves in the middle of an ice storm. Living in California, I didn't really know what an ice storm was, and I was later told this one was the worst Tennessee had seen in a hundred years. The temperature was well below zero and *everything* was covered with ice—every tree limb, every house, every bit of ground including our driveway and all the streets beyond. Everything! It looked like a sparkling fairyland. It felt like Siberia.

The weight of the ice on the trees caused big branches to break off and land on the power lines, knocking electricity out all over the city. We had no lights, no heat, and no phone. Coming from California, where anything below fifty degrees is considered life threatening, I seriously thought we might die there with the temperature well below zero.

We couldn't go anywhere, so we built a fire in the fireplace, huddled around it, and waited for the power and the telephone to come back on. They didn't that day. Nor the next. Or the next. And in that coldness, the fireplace didn't offer enough heat for us to move more than a few feet away from it without becoming painfully cold. On that first night, I stirred hot soup in a big pot that sat right on the fire and prayed, "Lord, help us. We need to know You're here."

I immediately sensed that instead of despairing over the misery of the situation, I was to embrace the experience and find His goodness in it. As I did, the results surprised me. I thanked God that He had kept us together as a family, instead of having someone stranded elsewhere and not knowing if they were safe. I was grateful that He had prepared us with a good supply of food and bottled water. I appreciated our fireplace and warm clothes that kept us from freezing. Though I might *feel* like a Siberian prisoner, I knew that I wasn't one. And I thought of the many people who experience this kind of existence as a way of life, only without the house, the food, the warm clothes, and the family. But most of all, I sensed God's presence there with us, and I praised Him for that. Our bodies were cold, but our hearts were warmed by the light He gave our souls.

Walking step by step with God requires embracing the moment for all it's worth. When you are tempted to become fearful, frustrated, uncertain, or panicked about what is happening in your life, stop and see that God is in it. And with Him, you have everything you need for this moment. Here and now.

It's amazing that when we open our eyes to the whole picture, we have a different perspective. The Bible says, "Open your eyes, and you will be satisfied with bread" (Proverbs 20:13). When we embrace Him, we see the blessings that are right in front of us. We can be content right where we are no matter what state we are in—literally or figuratively—because *He* is there (see Philippians 4:11).

Regardless of what your situation is at this moment, God has an abundance of blessings for you. Right where you are, God is working powerfully in your life. He wants you to close your eyes, call out His name, and say, "Lord, show me Your hand in my life." He wants you to sense His presence. He wants you to trust that when you are afraid, you can turn to Him and find His peace. When you are weary, you will find His strength. When you are empty, you will find His fullness. When you are sad, you will find His joy. And when you are in the middle of a raging storm, you will find His shelter and provision. But so often we become blinded by our circumstances, afraid of what's happening, easily discouraged, drawn toward bitterness, or quick to complain. And our first instinct is not to look for God in the midst of our circumstances.

"Why can't I have all the light I need right now, Lord?" we cry.

However, God knows that too much light can be hard to take. It can blind and confuse us. He prefers to give us just enough to keep us dependent on Him. In that way, He can teach us to take bigger steps of faith in order to prepare for what He is calling us to in the future.

When we have a deep and personal relationship with the Lord, our

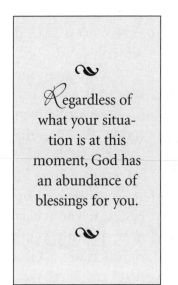

Regardless of what your situation is at this moment, God has an abundance of blessings for you.

difficult times are not the same as they are for people who don't have Him. For unbelievers, their dark and troubled times are without hope. Even for believers who don't understand all that God has for them, their difficult experiences are filled with fear and doubt instead of a sense of God's sustaining presence.

My friend Bill thought he knew the Lord well, but he actually had only a passing acquaintance with Him. Every Sunday morning he needed to get reacquainted with God because he had neglected to nurture that relationship on a daily basis. He didn't realize it was the most significant and life-transforming relationship he would ever have, so it didn't have a priority in his life. As a result, when he went through difficult times, his inability to hear God's voice and see His hand in the situation left him feeling powerless and defeated.

What would a marriage relationship be like if the husband and wife only saw each other for an hour each week? It would be shallow and inferior. It would be hopeless. It would probably not last. But many people have a similar relationship with God because they don't spend quality time with Him. They don't bring Him into their daily life and experiences. They don't look for Him in the midst of their difficulty and need.

I remember one particular time of great need in my life when I felt deeply lonely. It was the kind of loneliness that is so severe it brings physical pain as well as emotional agony. Because my lonely childhood had turned into a lonely adulthood, I always feared that loneliness would become a way of life for me. Even after I became a believer and experienced healing for the layers of emotional pain I had, it never occurred to me to ask God to heal my aloneness. Actually, I thought it could only be taken away by the right person. One night, however, I was so overwhelmed that I turned to God. I lifted my arms and cried, "Lord, why must I always be lonely? What can I do to get rid of this pain? You have promised to supply all my needs, and I need You to take this loneliness away."

The moment I prayed, I felt the arms of God surround me in an unmistakable way. I know that may sound strange. It would have sounded strange to me, too, had I not experienced it. But even more amazing is the fact that I have never felt loneliness like that since, even though I have been every bit as alone at times.

I now see any sign of loneliness as a call from God beckoning me to spend time with Him. I know He is not *causing* my loneliness. Nor is He *ignoring* it. He *sees* it and wants to fill the empty places of my heart with His love. As I embrace Him in the moment, He is always there.

When you take the first step to embrace God in your circumstances, He will go the distance to embrace you.

No matter what is going on in your life, embrace the moment. Instead of becoming upset when things go wrong or something doesn't happen the way you planned, look for God in the situation. You'll see He hasn't forsaken you. You'll understand that you won't be suffering forever. When you embrace the heart of God in the nitty-gritty details of your life, you will find a oneness with Him you never dreamed possible. And you'll sense that He is in control and will not let you get off course. Whenever you feel angry, sad, depressed, or fearful, say, "God, reveal Yourself to me in this moment. What are You doing in my life that I am not seeing? If all things work together for good, then show me the good." When you're determined to see the good, you will find it.

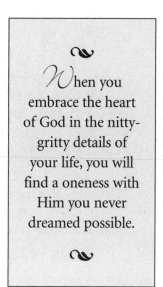

When you embrace the heart of God in the nitty-gritty details of your life, you will find a oneness with Him you never dreamed possible.

If God knows your thoughts (Psalm 94:11), your heart (1 Samuel 16:7), when you stand up and sit down (Psalm 139:2), and how many hairs you have on your head (Matthew 10:30), then He knows where you are at any given moment. He sees your circumstances. Just because *you* can't see anything ahead doesn't mean *He* can't. He *can* and *does*. He knows where you've been. He knows where you're headed. He knows where you are supposed to be going. And He knows how to get you there. If you have light for just the moment in which you find yourself, it is enough. It *must* be enough. For you have Him, and He is all you need.

Prayer Light

ord, You are everything to me. Thank You that I can walk each moment with You and not have to figure life out on my own. And when I come to a dark time, I can put my hand in Yours and depend on You as we walk through it together. I know that "the upright shall dwell in Your presence" (Psalm 140:13), and that's where I want to live. For in Your presence I will find healing, deliverance, love, peace, joy, and hope. Lord, help me to embrace the moments of my life that are hard to get my arms around. Enable my eyes to see You in them. Help me to always acknowledge the abundance of Your goodness to me. I lift to You the deepest struggles in my life. I trust You to open my eyes to see all You have for me in them. Reveal to me the fullness of it all. Thank You that I can be filled with the joy of Your presence in every step I take, because You have given me the light I need for whatever step I am on.

Footlights

For our light affliction, which is but for a moment,
is working for us a far more exceeding and
eternal weight of glory, while we do not look
at the things which are seen, but at the things
which are not seen. For the things which are
seen are temporary, but the things which
are not seen are eternal.

2 CORINTHIANS 4:17-18

In the day when I cried out, You
answered me, and made me bold
with strength in my soul.

PSALM 138:3

You know my sitting down and my rising up;
You understand my thought afar off.
You comprehend my path and my lying
down, and are acquainted
with all my ways.

PSALM 139:2-3

Though I walk in the midst of trouble,
You will revive me; You will stretch
out Your hand against the wrath
of my enemies, and Your right
hand will save me.

PSALM 138:7

FIVE

Dancing in the Footlights

We would never dream of hiking up a treacherous mountain path in the dark, with deep cliffs on one side that drop straight down for hundreds of feet and dangerous scorpions, snakes, wild animals, and patches of quicksand on the other. Why then would we even consider going through life that way?

Walking through each day without a clear guide, an accurate map, and a consistent light source is hazardous to your well-being. Fortunately, God's Word provides us with the tools and help that we need.

Unless the light of God's Word is shining on your steps, you are walking in dangerous territory.

After I came to know the Lord, I experienced times when it seemed like everything in my life was falling apart and I was walking blindly in darkness and confusion. But after only a few minutes of reading God's Word, clarity came to my mind. Confusion disappeared like fog in the presence of the sun. I gained a new perspective. Fear and anxiety left and peace took their place. God's voice spoke to my heart and I found clear direction again. It never failed!

That still happens every time I read the Scriptures.

People who say the Bible isn't relevant today obviously don't know the Author. They read it like a storybook or a history lesson, having no idea of the power behind it. They don't hear the Shepherd's voice because they have not become one of His sheep. But those of us who immerse ourselves in it, who press in deeper and deeper, know its power. We love His Word like a love letter that we read over and over because we desire to be close to the one who wrote it. We long to connect with and remember everything about that person. We want to understand how he thinks. We yearn to hear his voice again in our mind. We crave his touch. When we hunger for those same things from God, we learn to appreciate His love letter—the Bible—in that exact way.

Of course, if we don't love the person who sent us the love letter, it is meaningless. It holds no life for us. The key to receiving the full message in God's love letter is to love God. Because I love Him, I hear His voice speaking to me when I read His Word. If I read it often, the words find residence in my heart and bring me life.

> ∾
>
> *T*hose of us who immerse ourselves in God's Word, who press in deeper and deeper, know its power. We love His Word like a love letter we read over and over.
>
> ∾

God's Love Letters Are a Guide

In the theater, lights at the front of the stage that are level with the performer's feet are called footlights. They act as a guide to help the actors know where to go and keep them from falling into the orchestra pit. God has provided footlights for us, too—to guide us as we walk and to keep us from falling into the pit.

When we read God's Word, it lights our path and keeps us sure-footed. "Thy Word is a lamp unto my feet, and a light unto my path" (Psalm 119:105 KJV) is more than just a line from a nice worship song. It is a way of life. Walking step by step with God can only be done successfully if we have God's footlights showing us the way.

Those of us who have read the Bible many times from cover to cover have to be careful not to fall into the trap of thinking that the light we had last year, last month, last week, or even yesterday is enough to keep us safely on the path today. I have done enough public speaking to know that most of my preparation has to be done in prayer and in the Word of God. On my own, I am not able to speak words that will transform anyone's life. Only the anointing power of God attending those words can bring them alive in the hearts of the people listening. If I believe that I can rely on last week's anointing and don't have to prepare in the Word of God for next week's talk, I will find my message lacking in the very thing people want to experience— the Lord's touch. And that means I don't just read the Bible to prepare for the message. I also must feed on God's Word to prepare my soul and spirit.

A miner will never go down into a dark mine without checking to make sure the light on his cap has sufficient power to last the entire time he's down there. We need to be that diligent about God's Word. We can't just read it once from cover to cover and then be finished like we can with any other book. The light we receive from God's Word must be renewed, revitalized, and solidly reestablished daily. When God's truth is renewed in us each day, it becomes like *our* miner's light. As we look in the direction God is leading us, we are better able to see where we are going. "The law of his God is in his heart; none of his steps shall slide" (Psalm 37:31). In order to take it in so deeply that it becomes a part of us, we have to open the Bible and say, "Lord, speak to me today and show me what I need to know." Then we must read until our light is recharged.

God can speak to you from any page of His Word.

God's Love Letter Is a Weapon

When Satan came to tempt Jesus in the wilderness, Jesus spoke the Word of God to refute everything Satan said. Jesus told him that we live "by every word that proceeds from the mouth of God" (Matthew 4:4). If God's own Son refuted the devil in that way, shouldn't we do the same? Who among us are not susceptible to lies and temptations? Who does not get blinded by his or her own prejudices? Who never faces a battle and doesn't need a spiritual sword with which to slay the enemy? Only God's Word in our mind, on our heart, and out of our lips will burn away the darkness of untruth and arm us with a double-edged sword more powerful than any weapon the opposition can use against us. Who does not need that?

During times of great anxiety I have quoted passages from God's Word that dissolved my fear immediately. I liberally sprinkle Scriptures throughout my prayers for others, and I see them bolster faith like nothing else can. When I'm aware that my children are being threatened by an evil influence, I will speak the Word of God over them in prayer to see them released. There are no strongholds of the enemy that can prevail against God's Word.

> *O*nly God's Word in our mind, on our heart, and out of our lips will burn away the darkness of untruth and arm us with a double-edged sword more powerful than any weapon the opposition can use against us.

God's Love Letter Is a Message of Hope

There are no times so hopeless in our lives that God's Word will not shed light on the situation and bring us comfort. I've known many parents who have used the Word of God to combat the hopelessness they felt about the actions of their teenagers. They went into the child's room and simply read Scriptures out loud. Not only did hope rise in their own hearts, but they saw changes in their children happen soon after—even if the child was not there to hear it.

If you find yourself struggling with hopelessness, loss, sickness, or temptation, make God's Word an ongoing presence in your life. Hook up to it like an IV and let it flow continuously through your spiritual veins. Its light will burn hopelessness out of your life. "Whatever things were written before were written for our learning, that we through the patience and comfort of the Scriptures might have hope" (Romans 15:4). Don't let yourself even consider constructing a life without using God's Word as a power tool. In fact, make it your very foundation.

Anytime you feel like you are in the dark or on shaky ground, ask God to shed the light of His Word in your heart. Say, "send out Your light and Your truth! Let them lead me; let them bring me to Your holy hill" (Psalm 43:3). If you want to figure out how life works, read His instruction book. When you need to know where you're supposed to be going, His truth will aim you in the right direction, illuminate your way, and keep you from getting off the path.

Hunger for God's Word like food. Thirst for it like water. Soak in it like a jacuzzi. Put it on like a garment. Weave it into your soul so that it becomes part of the fabric of your life. When you do, you won't just be trudging up the trail. You will be dancing in the footlights.

Prayer Light

*L*ord, shine the light of Your Word on the path of my life today. Make it a lamp for my feet so that I do not stumble. Bring it alive in my spirit so that it illuminates my mind and soul. Let it be a guide for every decision I make, every step I take. Keep me from turning to the right or the left so that I will stay on the narrow path that leads to life. Help me daily to carve out time to be alone with You and to feed on Your Truth. "Oh, how I love Your law! It is my meditation all the day" (Psalm 119:97). Open my eyes to see new treasure every time I read or hear it. Speak to me and comfort my heart. Make Your Word come alive in me and use it to nourish my soul and spirit like food does for my body. Align my heart with Yours and give me revelation and guidance so that I may know Your will for my life. Shine the lamp of Your truth where I am right now and show me the next step to take.

Footlights

The entrance of Your words gives light;
It gives understanding to the simple.

PSALM 119:130

Great peace have those who love Your law,
And nothing causes them to stumble.

PSALM 119:165

For the commandment is a lamp,
And the law a light;
Reproofs of instruction
are the way of life.

PROVERBS 6:23

Direct my steps by Your Word,
And let no iniquity have dominion over me.

PSALM 119:133

For the word of God is living and powerful,
and sharper than any two-edged sword,
piercing even to the division of soul
and spirit, and of joints and marrow,
and is a discerner of the thoughts and
intents of the heart.

HEBREWS 4:12

SIX

Paying Your Light Bill

When your light bill arrives, you might be able to come up with at least four reasons for not paying it:

1. "I don't have what it takes."
2. "I don't want to."
3. "I didn't know I had to."
4. "I forgot."

Which one of these do you think the electric company will accept as a legitimate excuse for not paying?

You guessed it! None of the above.

Which one of these same four reasons does *God* accept as a good excuse for not living in obedience to His ways?

Right again! None of the above.

It doesn't matter if we forget to do the right thing, don't know what the right thing is to do, openly rebel, or feel like we just don't have it in us to accomplish it. The consequence is still the same—*darkness.*

Often we find ourselves walking in the dark simply because we are not willing to pay the price for having the light.

The price God requires for enjoying the fullness of His light is living His way. Whenever we don't live the way God asks us to live, or do not do what He has specifically told us to do, we forfeit the abundance of what He has for us. We won't experience the awesomeness of God's power in our lives if we are not willing to meet His conditions for plugging into it.

Receiving God's salvation doesn't cost us anything. He paid the price for that. His love and grace, among other things, are free as well. But receiving *all* He has for us does not happen without meeting certain requirements on our part. When we don't meet them, we end up being like "those who leave the paths of uprightness to walk in the ways of darkness" (Proverbs 2:13). In order to enjoy the *fullness* of His light, we have to walk in obedience to His ways. Usually we know when we are rebelling against God's laws. But sometimes our disobedience happens with such subtlety that we're not even aware of it.

When I was fourteen, I lived not far from the ocean in Southern California. One day I went to the beach with my

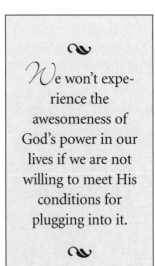

We won't experience the awesomeness of God's power in our lives if we are not willing to meet His conditions for plugging into it.

friend and her family. Because my friend and I were both good swimmers, no one was concerned when she and I ventured out in a little deeper water. Our peaceful floating was interrupted by a riptide, which began as a subtle undercurrent that we could not see or feel. In fact, we didn't notice it at all until we looked to shore and realized we were dangerously far out. We immediately tried to swim back, but the more effort we put forth, the further away from the beach we were carried. The tide was way too strong for us to swim against, and our sense of powerlessness was frightening.

Fortunately, there was a very long pier somewhat nearby, and as we were carried out beyond it we signaled to a fisherman standing on the end. He understood that we needed help and ran to tell the lifeguards. By that time we could see my friend's parents standing in the distance at water's edge, waving frantically for us to come back to shore.

The lifeguards arrived not a moment too soon for our pounding hearts and brought us safely back, where we fell in an exhausted heap on the sand. From our perspective on the shore, we were utterly amazed that we had been carried so far into dangerous territory without even realizing what was happening.

That's the way our lives are. The cares of the world, the influence of the ungodly, laziness, busyness, obsessions, ignorance of God's ways, or our own unsubmitted hearts, can be like a subtle riptide that carries us off course until one day we find that we are so far away from where we should be that we can't get back without help. Failure to be alert to the direction we are moving in is dangerous. And we don't have to be in open rebellion to get off course. All it takes is neglect in one small area of obedience and a subtle drift begins without our even noticing.

The Bible says that people who do *not* love God and who willfully do things their own way, for their own pleasure and with no regard for what it does to others or what God says about it, are called wicked and will find themselves in utter darkness. To them, what light they have is even dark. "The light of the wicked indeed goes out, and the flame of his fire does not shine" (Job 18:5). God withholds light from people who do not love or obey Him, but His light is placed in the path of those who live rightly. "Light is sown for the righteous . . ." (Psalm 97:11).

You and I are not the wicked God speaks of in His Word. But when we don't live the way He asks us to, we sacrifice much of the light we could enjoy. We don't experience the degree of His protection, guidance, and answers to prayer that we otherwise would. We forfeit certain blessings when we are not willing to do the things that must precede them.

When We Obey God, We Are Protected

Noah was called to build the ark because God said, "I have seen that you are righteous" (Genesis 7:1). Noah's righteousness ultimately saved him and his family from destruction. We can end up in the most wonderful places in our lives, places we wouldn't have thought to go on our own, simply because God sees our heart to live His way. When we love Him enough to obey what He asks, we come under the covering of His protection. When we don't, we come *out* from under it and drift further and further away from the shores of safety and blessing.

We can find ourselves in the wrong place at the wrong time simply because we didn't do what God was telling us to do, or we neglected to ask Him what we were supposed to be doing before we made decisions. Or perhaps we asked Him, but we failed to wait for an answer before we went ahead and did what we wanted to do. So much grief can be avoided by living God's way.

When We Obey God, We Hear His Voice

The more we obey God, the clearer we hear Him speaking to our heart. The more we hear God speaking to our heart, the more we want to obey Him. The more we obey, the more He can teach us of His ways, His truth, and

His nature. "His secret counsel is with the upright" (Proverbs 3:32).

After I became a Christian, I was not able to clearly hear God's direction for my life until I cleaned out my house of all the occultic books, magazines, music, and artifacts I had collected before I became a believer. I had stopped all occult practices, but had unwittingly neglected specific directions in God's Word until one day I read, "Do not bring a detestable thing into your house, or you, like it, will be set apart for destruction" (Deuteronomy 7:26 NIV). Suddenly my eyes were opened to what should have been obvious, and I got rid of everything that was offensive to God. I wanted to separate myself from anything that separated me from Him, and when I did I was able to hear His voice speaking to my heart.

God reveals Himself to us in greater dimensions when we are doing what He has asked us to do.

Pastor Jack Hayford says, "Obedience is not a work that *earns* something from God. Obedience is a willingness to *learn* something from God. We need to ask God, "Where do I need to obey You, Lord? What do I need to learn today?"

When we are walking in obedience, we don't miss God's direction for our lives.

When We Obey God, We See Answers to Our Prayers

If you find you are not enjoying answers to your prayers, ask God to show you if you have neglected to be obedient to His ways in some area of your life. For the longest time I did not see any answers to my prayers

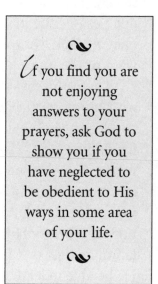

❧

*I*f you find you are not enjoying answers to your prayers, ask God to show you if you have neglected to be obedient to His ways in some area of your life.

❧

concerning my marriage. As a result, my husband and I went through some very dark times. When I finally realized that I had unforgiveness in my heart, I confessed it as God requires us to do and asked Him to set me free of it. After that, I prayed with a right heart, and I saw major answers to prayer that I had only dreamed about before. The light of God's restoration shined down on our relationship and brought much-needed healing.

The Bible says, ". . . whatever we ask we receive from Him, because we keep His commandments and do those things that are pleasing in His sight" (1 John 3:22). There is a direct correlation between obedience and answered prayer. Oswald Chambers says, "Intellectual darkness comes through ignorance; spiritual darkness comes because of something I do not intend to obey." [1]

When We Obey God, We Can Be Led by Him

Whatever we are passionately devoted to in our life will mold and control us. Whether it be the dictates of a trend-setting magazine or the catalogues of the rich, if the lust of our flesh or the pride of life is more important to us than obeying God, we will be overly influenced by the things we want or the image of who we want to be.

There are ways that are right and ways that are not and we cannot confuse the two. "Woe to those who call evil good, and good evil; who put darkness for light, and light for darkness . . ." (Isaiah 5:20). The voices of false gods, no matter how dressed up, popular, or politically correct their message appears to be, will get us so far off the path that we will never be able to find it again without God's intervention. If we obey Him, He will give us the light of His revelation and get us where we need to go. If we don't, how will He be able to lead us?

God is not trying to be a dictator. He simply wants to show us how life works best. When we don't live His way, confusion enters in and disturbing things happen that otherwise wouldn't. God is saying to us, "If you will do this, I will do that." In whatever area He is asking us to obey, we can be sure He is trying to teach us something that will be for our benefit.

Obedience is not legalism. It does not discount God's grace. Legalism says, "You have to do it perfectly on your own." God's grace says, "You need to do it to make your life better, but God will help you and pick you up if you fall."

Ask God to show you if there are certain steps of obedience He wants you to take. He'll tell you. You can depend on it. When you come to a place where you trust Him so thoroughly that you will obey whatever He says, you'll find that obedience won't be a gut-wrenching misery; it will be a privilege. You'll obey because the rewards are great. You'll obey out of the desire to have nothing come between you and God. You'll obey because you'll pay any price to not have your light shut off.

———————— *Prayer Light* ————————

Lord, I thank You that You have given me all the light I need for this day. I want to experience everything You have for me, and I am willing to pay the price of obedience for it. So if there is any area in my life where I am not walking in full obedience to Your ways, show me. If You want me to do something that I am not doing, make me understand and enable me to accomplish it. Don't let me drift away. Pull me out of deep waters and rescue me from all that takes me from You. I lay down my will and surrender to Yours. I turn away from selfish claims to my own life in order to heed Your direction. Take any rebellion in me and expose it with Your truth. "Search me, O God, and know my heart; try me, and know my anxieties; and see if there is any wicked way in me, and lead me in the way everlasting" (Psalm 139:23-24). Lord, I choose this day to obey You because I know my life works best when I do. In the areas where obedience is hard for me, walk me through step by step. I don't want to do anything that would dim the light You have for my path.

Footlights

Unto the upright there arises light in the darkness;
He is gracious, and full of compassion, and righteous.

PSALM 112:4

He shall bring forth your righteousness as the light,
And your justice as the noonday.

PSALM 37:6

For everyone practicing evil hates the light
and does not come to the light, lest
his deeds should be exposed. But he
who does the truth comes to the light,
that his deeds may be clearly seen,
that they have been done in God.

JOHN 3:20-21

. . . Your judgments are like light that goes forth.

HOSEA 6:5

"Enter by the narrow gate; for wide is the
gate and broad is the way that leads to
destruction, and there are many who go in by it.
Because narrow is the gate and
difficult is the way which leads to life, and
there are few who find it."

MATTHEW 7:13-14

SEVEN

Standing in the Line of Fire

If we go running into enemy territory and get shot at, we're not exactly being attacked. If we open ourselves up to the consequences of not living God's way, we shouldn't be surprised if enemy arrows pierce our lives. We've gotten out from the safety of God's covering.

On the other hand, if we are on our home turf minding our own business and doing what we know is right in God's sight, and from out of nowhere we are shot at, then we know our enemy has targeted us. We are in his line of fire, and he has mounted an attack on us. When that happens, we must immediately draw near to God. Oswald Chambers says of those dark times of enemy attack, "The thing that preserves a man from panic is his relationship to God." [1]

When we consistently live close to God, we have the peace and confidence of knowing who is our enemy and Who is our Defender. That doesn't mean that going through the battle is easy. But the closer you walk with God, the easier it becomes. We always hope that God will lift us *above* our circumstances. And sometimes He does. But much of the time He walks us *through* them so we can learn a new dimension of His power.

When the Israelites were delivered out of Egypt by the mighty hand of God and set on a journey of many miracles, they were doing what God had directed them to do. Still, they found themselves backed into an inescapable corner, with the Red Sea before them and the entire Egyptian army thundering up behind. They cried out to Moses in fear, and he assured them that the dangers they saw facing them would not be seen again. "'Stand still, and see the salvation of the LORD, which He will accomplish for you today. . . . The LORD will fight for you, and you shall hold your peace'" (Exodus 14:13-14). Not only did God fight the battle for them by parting the waters of the Red Sea so the Israelites could walk across the bottom, He also took them across on dry land.

Dry land!

When God does a miracle, He does a complete work.

Even when the Egyptian soldiers followed the Israelites into the riverbed to attack them, the sea closed and drowned the entire army. The Israelites "did not gain possession of the land by their own sword, nor did their own arm save them; but it was Your right hand, Your arm, and the light of Your countenance, because You favored them" (Psalm 44:3).

When God goes to battle for someone, He doesn't stop until the enemy is destroyed.

God will do the same for us today. When we are up against a wall and, in our eyes, the enemy is giving us no means of escape, the Lord will open up a way out. God will fight the battle for us. Even if we lose all strength in the face of it, *His* strength will be manifested as He wipes out the threat and works complete deliverance. But because any opposition we face from the enemy has spiritual power behind it, the battle must first be fought in the spirit before victory will be seen in the flesh. That means we need to pray.

I remember one morning when an article appeared in a prominent newspaper that misrepresented my husband, Michael. The story cast him in a very bad light by associating him with a recording artist who was living a seriously ungodly lifestyle. It said that Michael, who is a record producer, had a close association with this person, and the implications were that Michael condoned the immoral choices that this artist had made. Neither of these things were true. Michael and I were very concerned, so we prayed about the situation, contacted the newspaper, and then began calling everyone we could think of who might be hurt by such lies.

We talked to a number of people, including the writer of the article, but soon realized there was no way we could possibly reach everyone we needed to in order to preserve Michael's reputation. So we began to battle in prayer. We declared that Satan could not destroy what God had built. We would stand with the Lord and watch Him fight the battle for us, just as Jehoshaphat had done in the Old Testament.

When Jehoshaphat realized that "a great multitude" was coming against him, he set himself to seek God. He stood in the middle of the believers and said, "O LORD God of our fathers, are You not God in heaven, and do You not rule over all the kingdoms of the nations, and in Your hand is there not power and might, so that no one is able to

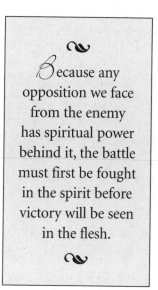

❧

*B*ecause any opposition we face from the enemy has spiritual power behind it, the battle must first be fought in the spirit before victory will be seen in the flesh.

❧

withstand You? . . . 'If disaster comes upon us—sword, judgment, pestilence, or famine—we will stand before this temple and in Your presence . . . and cry out to You in our affliction, and You will hear and save'" (2 Chronicles 20:6,9).

Jehoshaphat didn't say these things to remind God what He was capable of doing in case He had forgotten. He wanted to proclaim his own faith and inspire faith to rise up in the people. He knew that if they were reminded of the good things the Lord had done for them, they would be better equipped to believe God could save them.

Once the people humbly declared their dependence upon God, He spoke to them and said, "Do not be afraid nor dismayed because of this great multitude, for the battle is not yours, but God's" (2 Chronicles 20:15). God told them He would fight the battle for them. As Jehoshaphat and the people sang praise to the Lord, they won the battle *and* came away with more than they had before.

That's basically what happened to us in this situation with the newspaper article. We went to God, declared our dependence upon Him, reminded ourselves of His power and goodness, took a stance of faith in God's Word, and praised Him as we watched Him fight the battle for us. God miraculously shined the light of His grace and favor upon us and the entire matter dissipated. Of the countless people who read the article, no one to our knowledge ever gave it any credence. And we were left with a greater sense of God's power than we ever had before.

At the first sign of an enemy attack, go to the Lord and listen to what He tells you to do. He will guide you. No matter how dark it gets, He promises that "the light of the moon will be as the light of the sun, and the light of the sun will be sevenfold, as the light of seven days" (Isaiah 30:26). In other words, the light you have will be *magnified*.

Do you hear what He is saying?

In the midst of the battle, the light you have will not only never be put out, it will be brighter than it otherwise would have been.

That same passage of Scripture goes on to say, "You shall have a song as in the night when a holy festival is kept . . ." (Isaiah 30:29). That means that in the midst of what you are facing, your heart will have so much joy it's as if you are celebrating. You will have such a sense of His awesome presence that your soul will sing!

Much of the misery of being in a battle is thinking that we are all alone in it. I recall many times when I felt alone and afraid as I stood in the line of enemy fire, thinking I would surely be overcome by the waters of destruction swirling around me. But when I cried out to God and refused to doubt His goodness, He brought me through on dry ground and gave me peace and strength. The light I had was magnified, and He put a song in my heart. He will do that for you, too. No matter what your circumstances are, you can be sure that the Lord will be with you and help you successfully stand against whatever opposes you. When you walk with Him in the battle, you're never alone.

The hardest part about letting God fight your battle is that He sometimes waits until the eleventh hour so you will have no doubt of where the power is coming from. If that happens to you, hide yourself in Him and refuse to lose faith in His ability to come to your defense. "In returning and rest you shall be saved; in quietness and confidence shall be your strength" (Isaiah 30:15). Rest in the security of your Heavenly Father's

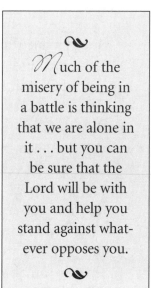

❧

*M*uch of the misery of being in a battle is thinking that we are alone in it . . . but you can be sure that the Lord will be with you and help you stand against whatever opposes you.

❧

arms until you see His power transform your circumstances.

The moment you realize you are standing in the line of fire, recognize who your enemy is and run to your Protector. Take His hand and He will show you moment by moment what you are to do. Put on the armor of God—prayer, praise, obedience, perseverance, peace, and faith. Throw a party in the Lord's presence and celebrate the victory He has for you, even before you see its manifestation. Let the song of praise and deliverance rise in your heart and sing it on the mountaintop of your soul as you watch the power of God defeat the enemy on your behalf. No matter how dark the night of your circumstances gets, remember that you still have a light. It comes from Him. It's in you and no enemy can ever put it out.

―――――――――― *Prayer Light* ――――――――――

*T*hank You, Lord, that You are my defender. You are more powerful than any plan the enemy has against me. Thank You that You will never leave or forsake me, and that You are always strong in my behalf. "I will lift up my eyes to the hills—from whence comes my help? My help comes from the LORD, who made heaven and earth" (Psalm 121:1-2). No matter what happens, I will look to You to deliver me from the hand of all that opposes me. I know that because I put my trust in You, You will be my shield (Proverbs 30:5). And I will not fear what man can do to me. "Lead me, O LORD, in Your righteousness because of my enemies; make Your way straight before my face" (Psalm 5:8).

In myself I don't have what it takes to establish a formidable defense. I cannot protect myself and all I care about from the weapons of the enemy. But the enemy's strength is nothing to You. And no weapon formed against me shall prosper (Isaiah 54:17). I know You have armed me with strength for the battle and will keep me safe (Psalm 18:39). Help me to "cast off the works of darkness, and . . . put on the armor of light" (Romans 13:12). Cause a song of deliverance to rise in my heart and I will sing praise to Your glory as You fight the battle for me. I will walk with You through the enemy's attack, knowing that Your light on my path signals my certain victory.

Footlights

Do not rejoice over me, my enemy;
When I fall, I will arise;
When I sit in darkness,
The LORD will be a light to me.

MICAH 7:8

. . . be strong in the Lord and in the power of His might.
Put on the whole armor of God, that you may be
able to stand against the wiles of the devil. For
we do not wrestle against flesh and blood,
but against principalities, against powers,
against the rulers of the darkness of this age,
against spiritual hosts of wickedness in the
heavenly places. Therefore take up the whole
armor of God, that you may be able to withstand in the evil day, and having
done all, to stand.

EPHESIANS 6:10-13

Keep me as the apple of Your eye;
Hide me under the shadow of Your wings,
From the wicked who oppress me,
From my deadly enemies who surround me.

PSALM 17:8-9

EIGHT

Seeing What's Right with This Picture

Have you ever found yourself angry, upset, or devastated when things didn't turn out as you'd hoped or planned? Next time that happens, look deeply into the situation and ask God to give you a new perspective.

We can usually find another way to view our situation beyond how we initially see it. Because we walk in the light of the Lord, blessings abound for us in each moment. Sometimes, though, we have to deliberately look for them. God's light does not blind us, but we can be blind to God's light. We don't always see the *whole* truth. Sometimes we see everything *but* the truth.

My daughter, Mandy, and I have developed a plan for seeing the truth whenever something goes wrong. We look at the situation and ask, "What's *right* with this picture?" We pray for God to show us how what we think of as a negative situation is actually a positive one. We take even the smallest issue and reverse it. We examine the flip side. This process can become funny as we stretch to find every positive aspect, but it keeps us protected from the cynical, peless, and bitter attitudes that can creep into our personalities.

For example, Mandy had a car accident when she was sixteen. Fortunately, the lady who hit her apologized and admitted to the police and the insurance company that she was entirely to blame. As the cars were towed away, I asked my very shaken daughter what was right with this picture.

"Well, no one was hurt," she replied.

"Yes, that's the best thing," I said. "But there is another good thing. This accident is going to make you a better driver because now you realize that even when you're doing everything right, bad things can still happen. You'll be extra aware of other drivers and how important it is to pray for God's protection as you travel. What you have learned from this might be the very thing that saves your life some day."

This is not just positive thinking or trying to make good things happen with your thoughts. This is seeing things from God's perspective and letting Him show you the truth. That means *finding* the light in what seems to be a dark situation. It's knowing that, because you have invited God into every step of your life, you can find His light there no matter how dark it seems.

"Embracing the moment" is embracing God and finding Him in the moment. "Seeing what's right with this picture," on the other hand, is searching for the truth and seeing reality from God's perspective. It's being willing to let go of our determination to see things through our own tunnel vision.

Have you ever known people who are so set on believing something bad about another person that

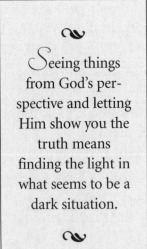

Seeing things from God's perspective and letting Him show you the truth means finding the light in what seems to be a dark situation.

they refuse to hear anything good? They make a case against that person and everything that person says or does is twisted to support the case. Nothing will change their minds. Not reason. Not God. This is the same kind of hard-nosed narrow-mindedness that feeds prejudice, gossip, jealousy, and hatred. Seeing what's right with this picture counteracts that tendency. It may be a lighthearted way of approaching a very dark-spirited issue, but it's a good place to start.

Let me give you some more examples. When my family and I were on a plane coming home from vacation, we flew through severe turbulence. The plane rocked and shook so violently that everyone on board was afraid. After it was over and people could actually talk again, we looked to find what was good about the situation. We decided that the best part, of course, was that we landed safely. Another good thing was that it forced all of us who were believers on the flight—and probably non-believers as well—to pray fervently. (Actually, *desperately* might be a more accurate word choice.) When we found out later that the turbulence we flew through was the edge of a serious tornado that hit Alabama, we realized that if we had not been praying at that very time for God to calm the storm, there might have been even more damage and fatalities on the ground than there were.

In another instance, I spoke to a young man named Mark who had always disdained his father's success because he only saw it as something he had to live up to. In Mark's mind, it had become such an impossible task that he felt defeated by it. When he was able to flip the picture over and see what was good about the situation, Mark gained a completely different perspective. He saw the advantages of having a father who was respected and gave his family a good name. He saw the benefits of the good schooling his father was able to provide. He recognized the positives of having a hardworking father for a role model. Together, we found many more positives than negatives. This exercise changed Mark's whole attitude, which led to great healing in his relationship with his dad.

In yet another example, a friend of ours named Jonathan was laid off from work and was initially feeling very defeated about it. But instead of letting his frustration turn into bitterness, he looked to see what was right with this picture. Jonathan gradually recognized it as an opportunity to help his wife, Lisa, establish a new business she had been wanting to start now that their children were grown. Instead of falling into depression, he worked hard for her. The business soon took off and became one of the most successful companies of its kind in town. Lisa would never have been able to do what she did without Jonathan's help. What seemed like a disaster at first actually was a blessing. What appeared to be a dark time became a time flooded with light. If Jonathan had complained and blamed God, refusing to see the situation from His perspective, things probably would have turned out quite differently.

This may be a big shock to you—I know it was to me—but often when we think something unfortunate is happening to us, it's actually an answer to a prayer we have prayed. Only the answer didn't manifest the way we thought it should, so we failed to recognize it. That's why seeing what's right is entirely a matter of having God's perspective.

Jennifer had been praying faithfully for her troubled relationship with her husband, David. When the company David had been working for was downsized, he found himself without employment for what turned out to be ten months. This kind of a turn could have destroyed an already ailing marriage. But instead of sinking into despair, Jennifer asked God to show her the truth about the situation. God revealed it was *not* true that her husband's career, as well as their marriage, was finished as they had both feared. The truth was that God had a great path ahead for them, but they couldn't walk it if they were crippled by a broken marriage. God was giving them time together to repair it.

Instead of letting this situation become a disaster that ripped them apart, David and Jennifer wisely took advantage of the opportunity to seek Christian counsel, be with godly friends, and spend time together doing the things they never had time to do before. Their marriage healed miraculously, and David eventually found more fulfilling work than he had ever had before.

Often we pray for something and don't even recognize the answer to our own prayers when we receive it, because it does not happen the way we thought it would.

When I read about God leading the Israelites out of Egypt after many unmistakable miracles, I was amazed at how they continually grumbled and complained and failed to see how God was taking care of them.

What is the matter with these people that they can't see the answers to their own prayers? I thought.

Then I realized we are all just like them. God is in the middle doing something great for us and, because we are not as comfortable as we'd like to be, we don't recognize the good things He has put in our lap. "Eyes they have, but they do not see" (Psalm 115:5).

How many blessings must we have forfeited because we resisted God when we should have been thanking Him?

> ∾
>
> God is in the middle of doing something great for us and, because we are not as comfortable as we'd like to be, we don't recognize the good things He has put in our lap.
>
> ∾

Look at your life right now. Is there anything that worries or upsets you? If so, say, "Lord, show me what's right with this picture. What is the truth in this moment? Help me to see it from Your perspective." You'll be amazed at what God reveals.

If your attitude is one of gratefully searching for God's truth and goodness in any situation, it will change your life. You'll never see things the same way again. No matter what happens, you'll be able to say, "This was the LORD's doing; it is marvelous in our eyes" (Psalm 118:23). What we're really talking about here is an issue of trust. It's basically believing that God is good and he desires the best for you. "Oh, taste and see that the LORD is good; blessed is the man who trusts in Him!" (Psalm 34:8). Give God the benefit of your trust and you'll see that you are standing in more light than you ever dreamed possible.

Prayer Light

*L*ord, I lift to You the situations of my life that concern me. I lay my worries before You and ask for Your mighty intervention to show me what's right when I can only see what's wrong. I am determined to see the good, so help me not to be blinded by my own fears, doubts, wants, and preconceived ideas. I ask You to reveal to me Your truth in every situation. Give me Your perspective. Bless me with the ability to understand the bigger picture and to distinguish the valuable from the unimportant. When something seems to go wrong, help me not to jump to negative conclusions. Enable me to recognize the answers to my own prayers. I trust You to help me see the light in every situation.

Footlights

And we know that all things work together
for good to those who love God,
to those who are the called
according to His purpose.

ROMANS 8:28

I would have lost heart, unless I had believed
That I would see the goodness of the LORD
In the land of the living.

PSALM 27:13

Turn away my eyes from looking at worthless things,
And revive me in Your way.

PSALM 119:37

Open my eyes, that I may see
Wondrous things from Your law.

PSALM 119:18

This is the day the LORD has made;
We will rejoice and be glad in it.

PSALM 118:24

NINE

Testing, One, Two, Three

Remember how each time you took a test in school you had to study hard so you'd know the material and be able to pass the test? The purpose of the test was for the teacher to determine how much you knew and, consequently, what grade you would receive. The more you knew, the better your grade.

God's tests are not like school tests. First of all, He already knows how much we know. The test is not for Him. It's for us. God's test helps us clearly see what we're made of. It teaches us about ourselves and about God. The test itself is part of our learning process.

The results of the tests God gives us, depending on our attitude in the midst of the testing, will determine whether we are refined like gold by the process or become cold and hard like steel. It won't necessarily be how much we know that counts, but what we do with the knowledge we've got. It's *how* we take the test.

In the tests that God gives us, we receive no grade. We will either pass, or we'll have to keep taking it until we get right. We have two choices with regard to God's tests. We can resist God, have a bad attitude, and try to run from it. Or we can embrace *Him* in it and welcome His perfecting hand in our lives. Our reaction will determine the outcome.

The most miserable times in my life as a believer have been during what I see now were periods of testing. And they came just before the most significant breakthrough of God's light. The good news is that the more challenging the test, the more monumental the reward waiting for us on the other side of it—*if* we react to it in the right way.

We are often put to our most difficult test just before the greatest work of God in our lives is about to be accomplished.

I remember one particular time when my husband and I were going through a serious financial crunch and it looked like we would have to sell our house. I was pregnant and seriously ill and did not see how I could possibly find another place to live, make the move, and still live through it. My husband and I were before God daily trying to determine if this was an enemy attack, or if we had done something wrong, or if we were being put to the test. The only answer we received was to be still and know that the Lord was God.

Although the crisis seemed to go on forever, it actually lasted only a few months. During that period God showed us how to not do anything but praise Him in the midst of what was happening. When we submitted fully to the Lord, even though it wasn't our first reaction, we clearly saw how utterly dependent we were upon Him. It was exactly what we needed to learn in order to navigate the waters that were ahead for us in the coming years. Our financial crisis was resolved when people who owed my husband money for work he had done finally paid him. We were able to keep our house, and the Lord poured blessings upon us that I doubt we would have enjoyed had we not gone through that time of testing. We knew the rewards were from Him.

The Bible's story of Job is important because the magnitude of Job's suffering in his time of testing is unimaginable. It is the worst case scenario. He lost everything, including his children and his health. Although he suffered such agony, he never doubted or turned against God. His reward for faithfulness was that "the LORD blessed the latter days of Job more than his beginning" (Job 42:12).

I know that most of us feel we would just as soon not be quite so blessed in our latter days and forget the whole testing thing. But we aren't given that choice. God decides the time, place, and manner of testing. No matter what the test entails, God wants us to have unflinching faith in the midst of it, just like Job had.

After God performed so many miracles to deliver the Israelites from the hand of their enemies and they still continued to doubt Him, He then took them into the wilderness and there He tested them (Exodus 15:25). He let them go without water for three days. Now God knew they needed water and could have easily provided it for them. But they didn't ask. They didn't pray. They complained. And that was part of the test. God wanted them to ask. He wanted them to be dependent on Him for everything. When Moses cried out to God on their behalf, God said that if the people would listen to Him and do what He commanded, He would meet all their needs. So they listened, and obeyed. They got their water. And were content. That is, until the next crisis.

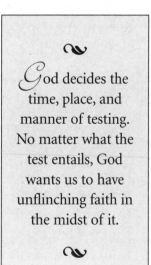

God decides the time, place, and manner of testing. No matter what the test entails, God wants us to have unflinching faith in the midst of it.

Instead of learning something from the water situation, the Israelites complained again about their lack of food. God was not trying to starve them. He knew they needed food, and He wanted to provide it for them. Only He wanted them to come to Him and rely on *Him* for it. Once more, Moses prayed and God provided. But this time, God provided only what was needed for that day. He desired that they trust Him for everything, each day that they needed it. He wanted them to learn to walk with just enough light for the step they were on.

Does this sound at all familiar? Can you think of anyone who wants to get to the Promised Land, but doesn't want to do what's necessary to make the trip? Are you aware of a person who desires to have everything he needs, but is not willing to give up anything to get it? Can you imagine someone who believes she should have already arrived without having to trust God for every step to get there? Can you think of anyone who would even consider trying to pass a test without having taken it? So can I. I think we all can.

God puts us through different kinds of tests. But He gives us three major tests that we will all have to take at one time or another.

Test One: God Tests Our Heart

"I know also, my God, that You test the heart and have pleasure in uprightness" (1 Chronicles 29:17).

The famous fall that pride always goes before is something God allows in order to purify us from our inclination to be full of ourselves. Just when we have enough arrogance to think we can live one moment without Him, God searches our heart for humility. If found wanting, He allows us to hit rock bottom and gain a new perspective. Looking up. And this is exactly what we need if we've been looking down for too long. God doesn't give this kind of test to torture us. He does it so our hearts can be purified and we can see *Him*. "Blessed are the pure in heart, for they shall see God" (Matthew 5:8).

Six years ago, I had a serious fall that broke two bones in my ankle and tore the ligaments on both sides. As I lay in bed for weeks, unable to put pressure on my foot even in a cast, I had plenty of time to pray and listen. I soon realized that God had been trying to get my attention for some time in order to make certain major changes in my life, but until I was flat on my back in pain I didn't want to listen. It was in this predicament that God showed me clearly we were to move from Los Angeles to Tennessee. My heart had to be tested in the fire and it was painful. Would I do what God wanted, or what I wanted? Ultimately, God's purposes were accomplished and we ended up in the right place at the right time.

Test Two: God Tests Our Faith

"Count it all joy when you fall into various trials, knowing that the testing of your faith produces patience" (James 1:2-3).

One of the most profound times our faith is tested is when we are struggling with our finances. Few things are more upsetting than the prospect of losing your home, not having enough food, or not being able to pay your bills. This is especially frightening when it involves a family with dependent children. But learning to walk in the provision God gives us for the day in which we find ourselves opens our eyes to see how we must depend on Him for everything. It forces us to live in God's presence in a deeper way as we look to Him to work daily miracles on our behalf.

When our faith is tested during these times, our response to it is revealing. Do we trust Him to provide, or do we get angry and take it out on others? Do we view this as a time that God wants us to draw closer to Him, or do we see it as the termination of our future? Do we understand that God is testing us in order to prepare us for what He is going to do in our lives, or do we believe He is forsaking us? Will we lose patience in this time, or will we grow in faith? The answers we give to these questions are the keys to passing the test.

Test Three: God Tests Our Obedience

"'In this way I will test them and see whether they will follow my instructions'" (Exodus 16:4 NIV).

My own children have always determined the amount of privileges they enjoyed by how obedient they were to the rules we laid down in our home. If they didn't obey the rules, we didn't extend the rewards. Of course, we were committed to feed, clothe, educate, shelter, and love them no matter what they did. But the extra blessings they enjoyed over and above those things depended on their obedience. For example, when they were teenagers we asked them to do their own laundry and clean their rooms. If they didn't obey, we knew they were therefore not responsible enough to drive a car. Of course they could live without driving a car, but their joy would certainly not be as full.

God views us much the same way. He requires specific things of us and tests us to see if we will do them. If we don't, He doesn't withhold His love, provision, and protection from us. But He wants to bless us in so many more ways, and He can't unless we are completely submitted to Him. Moses told the Israelite people, "'God has come to test you, so that the fear of God will be with you to keep you from sinning'" (Exodus 20:20 NIV). God also says that "fire will test the quality of each man's work" (1 Corinthians 3:13 NIV). None of us want to go through the fire of being tested, but we can eliminate much of our misery by being quick to respond to what God asks us to do.

A frequent question we all have is, *How do I know if what I am going through is an enemy attack, a result of my own disobedience, or one of God's tests?* The way to determine the answer is to ask God, "Lord, is this from the enemy?" If He doesn't show us that it is, then we should not automatically blame everything on the devil and thereby absolve ourselves of any responsibility. We're still made of flesh no matter how spiritual we get. We can all be tempted to think, say, or do things that are not right in the sight of God. That's why we must also say, "Lord, have I done anything to cause this?" He will reveal it to you if you have. God doesn't keep our sins secret from us. If you still don't have an answer, say, "Lord, are You putting me to the test? If so, show me what I need to learn. Create in me a clean heart and a right spirit."

Don't fear the time of testing God takes you through. It doesn't have to be miserable. Think of it as a refining that will reveal anything amiss in your life and show you where changes need to be made. The only way God can lead you to where you've never been, and can't get to without Him, is to call you to a new place in your life that requires more purity of heart, more faith, and more obedience than you've ever known. Your reaction during this period will be revealing. Will you love Him above all else? Will you believe He is who He says He is and trust Him to provide for your needs? Will you do what He tells you to do? If you are fearful and bitter during the process, you delay the blessings God is waiting to rain on you. That's what the Israelites did, and they wandered around for forty years on a journey that should have taken just a few weeks. You don't want to do that.

Walking with just enough light for the step you're on in a time of testing is God's way of preparing you for the great things He has ahead. Ask Him to help you learn your lesson well.

———————— *Prayer Light* ————————

*L*ord, grow me up in Your ways and lead me in Your will. Help me to become so strong in You that I will not waver or doubt. Make me to understand Your Word and Your directions to me. "Test me, O LORD, and try me, examine my heart and my mind; for your love is ever before me and I walk continually in your truth" (Psalm 26:2-3 NIV). I want to pass successfully through any time of testing You bring me to so that I might be refined. I don't want to wander around in the wilderness, going over and over the same territory because I haven't learned the lesson. I pray that I will always have a teachable heart that recognizes Your hand in my life and soaks up Your instruction. Help me to trust Your timing. Establish in me an unwavering faith so I will know that when I walk with You, even the refining fire provides the perfect light for the step I'm on.

Footlights

You have tested my heart;
You have visited me in the night;
You have tried me and have found nothing;
I have purposed that my mouth
shall not transgress.

PSALM 17:3

. . . You, O LORD, know me;
You have seen me,
And You have tested my
heart toward You.

JEREMIAH 12:3

Praise our God, O peoples,
Let the sound of his praise be heard;
He has preserved our lives
And kept our feet from slipping.
For you, O God, tested us;
You refined us like silver.

PSALM 66:8-10 (NIV)

. . . I have refined you, but not as silver;
I have tested you in the furnace of affliction.

ISAIAH 48:10

I will bring the one-third through the fire,
Will refine them as silver is refined,
And test them as gold is tested.
They will call on My name,
And I will answer them.
I will say, "This is My people";
And each one will say,
"The LORD is my God."

ZECHARIAH 13:9

TEN

Knowing How to Pack for the Wilderness

When God is taking us to a place we've never been before, we envision that it's going to be better than where we are. And ultimately, that's true. But often we have to go through a wilderness to get there.

God has a purpose for the wilderness, but it's hard to see it when we're in it. It can be frightening if we don't know what to expect. The most frightening thing about it is the thought that this may be our final destination.

When God called my husband and me to leave Los Angeles and move to Tennessee, it was one of the most difficult things I had ever done in my life. I had to leave what I loved and what was familiar to me to go where everything seemed foreign. Not that one culture was better or worse than the other, but they were so different from each other—and from the rest of the world. It was like going from Mars to the moon. I hope that none of the good people of California and Tennessee will take offense to my analogy, but in *my* particular experience on this journey that God was taking *me* through, California was Egypt and Tennessee was the wilderness.

Even though there was a lot I did not miss about Los Angeles, there were many things I couldn't let go of. And even though Tennessee is probably one of the most beautiful places in the world and home to the kindest of people, so much was missing for me. I felt like an alien. And, just like the Israelites did when God led them out of Egypt, I grumbled and complained.

"Oh, for the meat and bread of Egypt!" the Israelites cried.

"Oh, for the fruits and vegetables of California!" I lamented.

"Oh, for some fish and a new pair of shoes like we had back home!" they complained.

"Oh, for the restaurants, amusement parks, and beaches I used to go to!" I moaned.

I knew God had clearly led us to Tennessee, so I was completely surprised to find myself this miserable. I thought that when God flies you out of Egypt, you touch down in the Promised Land. *Of course* I knew that the Israelites had to go through the wilderness, but they were a bunch of ungrateful complainers, weren't they?

"Lord, why did you bring me here to the middle of nowhere?" I grumbled. "I had a life in L.A."

I didn't know then that although the wilderness may seem like nowhere at the time, it is *somewhere* if that's where God wants you. For it's there He will prepare you for the good thing He is about to do in your life. It's there you will be thoroughly convinced that you won't get anywhere or accomplish anything lasting without Him.

It's not where we are in life that matters, but Who is with us.

The wilderness is where we are forced to leave behind the familiar, the comfortable, the past successes, the accomplishments, and the old bag of tricks that always worked before. The wilderness is where God takes us when He wants to get Egypt out of our hearts. He wants to separate us from all that we crave, so that all we crave is Him. Just as God wanted to get the taste for Egypt out of the Israelites' mouths, He wants to get the lust for certain comforts out of our appetites, too. It's not that He doesn't want us to ever be comfortable. It's just that He doesn't want us to *depend* on the comfortable. He wants us to depend on *Him*. He doesn't want us to love the comforts more than we love *Him*. When God aims us in a new direction, we have to let go of what we've known, be willing to embrace the unfamiliar, and trust that He will sustain us on the journey.

All great people of faith have traveled into the unknown at some point in their lives. How must Noah have felt when he gathered his family on board the ark before the floods came? Nothing like it had ever been built before. He didn't even know for sure that it would float. He had to leave all that was familiar to him, and he certainly did not know where he would end up. I'm sure his hand was in God's when the rains came and the fountains of the deep were released. Who could imagine the magnitude of such a flood? I'm certain Noah took each step clinging to God's every word of revelation. He knew God was in control of his life and had put him in the right place at the right time.

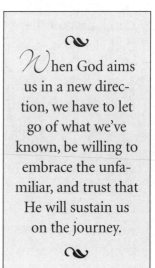

⁓

When God aims us in a new direction, we have to let go of what we've known, be willing to embrace the unfamiliar, and trust that He will sustain us on the journey.

⁓

That's exactly the place we want to be. That's the kind of assurance we must have. We need to be walking so close to the Lord that we hear His voice in the midst of any upheaval in our lives. We have to trust Him so thoroughly that we will follow Him wherever He leads us. We must walk perfectly within the revealed light God has given us, not running ahead, not lagging behind, not striving to go somewhere else.

When traveling in the wilderness, there is a good possibility that God will not reveal our final destination. He has a number of reasons for this. For one thing, if He did reveal where we were going, it wouldn't be such a walk of faith. Another reason is that the full magnitude of what's ahead is often too much for us to comprehend. We might get in God's way by thinking too small, or delay the process if we become doubtful. We also might have so many questions that we become paralyzed with fear waiting for the answers.

God took the Israelites through the wilderness because taking them the direct route meant they would have to fight the Philistines. "Then it came to pass, when Pharaoh had let the people go, that God did not lead them by way of the land of the Philistines, although that was near; for God said, 'Lest perhaps the people change their minds when they see war, and return to Egypt'" (Exodus 13:17). God knew that the Israelites would have been too afraid at that point to trust Him to fight their battles for them, so He took them on a different route.

Their wilderness experience could have been a much shorter one had their response to it been one of obedience and submission. But they wandered in the wilderness for years because they didn't get it. You and I won't have to do that because we *do* get it. We now understand that the reason God takes us through these wilderness times is because He wants us to learn a walk of faith whereby we trust Him for every step. We recognize that the wilderness is a place where God calls us to forsake what's comfortable and move into the unknown so He can guide us where we need to go.

The bread that God fed the Israelites in the wilderness was called manna. Every day they had to look for it and gather it. We, too, have to daily gather the manna God has for us. We have to seek God's presence and find the strength, joy, peace, and rest that nourishes and feeds our souls. We have to understand that in a place where there appears to be nothing, God will provide everything we need. The knowledge that all this is there for us in the wilderness is liberating. It frees us from having to be discontent. It frees us from striving to get out of the wilderness before it's time to leave. It frees us from trying to make things different than they are. It liberates us to allow God to do a new thing in us as He wills.

Just as God wanted the Israelite's allegiance, He wants yours, too. He also wants your attention, your trust, your mind, your soul, your body, and your obedience. In a word, He wants *you*. Don't deny Him that pleasure. Embrace the wilderness and say, "I want to be with You, Lord, even if that means staying in the wilderness until You're ready to bring me out." As Moses said, "'If Your Presence does not go with us, do not bring us up from here'" (Exodus 33:15).

God had the Israelites fill one jar with manna to keep in order to show future generations how He provided for them in the wilderness. Once

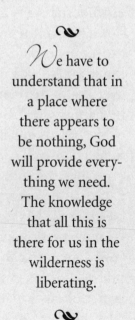

*W*e have to understand that in a place where there appears to be nothing, God will provide everything we need. The knowledge that all this is there for us in the wilderness is liberating.

you are out of the wilderness, don't forget it. Remember and talk about the goodness God showed you there, and how He sustained you and how you trust He will continue to do so. It will strengthen your faith and the faith of those around you.

My husband and I and our children frequently remind ourselves of how our lives have been blessed in Tennessee. Our wilderness time is over now and we're enjoying the milk and honey of the Promised Land. We love L.A., but don't long for it anymore. We know the wilderness is not a place; it's a spiritual growth process. In our case it was actually an answer to our own prayers. We followed the Lord, made it through the wilderness, and now the wilderness will always be a part of us because we don't ever want to let go of the priceless knowledge of God's goodness we gained there.

If you ever find that God is leading you into some kind of wilderness, my advice is to forget Egypt as quickly as you can. The comforts you once knew will not be there, so don't expect them. And don't lament over what you're missing or think you're lacking. Give yourself five minutes of grief over them, then let them go so you can enjoy the journey. Be happy where God has you. No one ever gets out of the wilderness as quickly as they would like to anyway, so refuse to feel deprived.

When traveling in the wilderness, learn to seek the abundance of the moment. Ask God to open your eyes to all the blessings He has for you there. As you see each one, let them become a refreshing spring. Soak them into the dry pores of your soul, drink them into the parched areas of your spirit, praise Him for every one, and feel that solid ground at the center of His will. Oh, and remember to pack lightly. I'd say take the Word of God, a measure of patience, a garment of praise, a pair of knee pads for those fervent prayer times, and an open vessel to hold the living water God is going to pour out on you. That's all you can manage on that path, anyway—especially in the kind of light you're going to have.

——————————— *Prayer Light* ———————————

*L*ord, I am at home wherever You are. If you call me into the wilderness, I will embrace it because You are there with me. Help me to not walk in fear or doubt, but in faith. Shine Your light on the path You have for me to travel, for I know that all my days are in Your hands. Forgive me when I grumble or have less than a grateful heart about where I am right now. I realize that my attitude will have a direct bearing on whether I wander around in circles, coming back to the same place over and over, or whether I get through to the Promised Land You have for me. Help me to trust You for every step. Enable me to see all the blessings that are right here in this moment. I trust that Your grace is sufficient for this day, and each day that follows.

Footlights

"If anyone serves Me, let him follow Me;
and where I am, there My servant will be also.
If anyone serves Me, him My Father will honor."

JOHN 12:26

"Whoever desires to come after Me,
let him deny himself,
and take up his cross,
and follow Me."

MARK 8:34

"My Presence will go with you,
and I will give you rest."

EXODUS 33:14

"My sheep hear My voice,
and I know them,
and they follow Me."

JOHN 10:27

Blessed are the people who know the joyful sound!
They walk, O LORD, in the light
of Your countenance.

PSALM 89:15

ELEVEN

Surrendering Your Dreams

Most of us have experienced a time when our lives appear to be standing still. No matter how hard we work, it seems like every door is closed and no new ones are opening. Often that's because we have an image in our mind of what we *want* to be happening, and when we see that it isn't we think *nothing* is happening.

We can end up in a stagnant wilderness of frustration and confusion if we have made idols out of our dreams.

God wants us to dream. He puts dreams in our heart for His purposes. But in our dreaming, He doesn't want us to exclude *Him*. God's Word says we will perish if we don't have a vision, but the vision we have must be His. If we don't have a vision from *Him*, then we don't have a vision that will ever be realized.

I know a young man who had a dream of the girl he wanted to marry. He had her every detail figured out, from the way she looked to the way she talked and thought. However, he could never find anyone who lived up to his dream. And I didn't have the heart to tell him that there was no girl on earth who could. Or would want to, for that matter. After years of frustrated searching, he was finally led to the feet of the Lord where he surrendered that dream to God. Right after he did, he met his future wife and married her within that year. When I met her, I found it amusing that she was nothing like the dream girl he had previously described to me. But she was perfect for him because she was the one God had chosen.

God wants us to surrender our dreams because we can't be led by Him if we are chasing after a dream of our own making. And He wants us to surrender *all* of them. That way He can tell us which of them are from Him and in line with *His* will, and which of them are ours and born out of *our* will. If they are only our dreams and visions and not His, we will experience a lifetime of unfulfillment and strife trying to make them happen. Even if the dream in your heart *is* from God, you still won't see it fulfilled until you give it to Him. The dream has to be realized *His* way.

Every fall in California we would cut our rosebushes back to nearly nothing. For about four months they looked like pathetic little dead sticks from which nothing could ever possibly grow again. But when spring came, they blossomed and bloomed profusely. First they grew hundreds of little buds. Then one by one they opened and burst into all shades of pink, purple, yellow, burgundy, and white. Abundant, fragrant, breathtaking, life-giving flowers that people driving or walking by would stop to admire. That's what God wants to do with us. He wants us to be His rose garden. He wants us to have beauty and purpose, and to give out a lifegiving fragrance to those around us. But first comes the pruning. First comes the period of dead-looking sticks.

When God wants to make changes in our lives, and we're willing to let Him, He starts by cutting away all that is unnecessary. In this process, He strips from us everything that could hinder our future growth, in order to prepare us to bring forth good fruit. Our life may look barren during that time, but God is actually freeing us from anything that does not bring forth life. This process of surrendering all to the Lord, especially our dreams and desires, is called pruning.

My husband, who has been a successful musician for thirty years, once knew that God was asking him to lay down his music for a time. He was twenty years old and already a professional piano player and writer when the Lord made it clear to Him that music was an idol in his life. He had to surrender his dream of ever playing or writing again. After two years of not doing anything in the music field—he didn't even practice the piano during that time—God gave him back the dream because it now had a different place in his heart. He went through the test, he endured the wilderness, he surrendered his dream, and he saw it resurrected. I don't believe his success would have been as far-reaching, or have had the longevity it has had, if he hadn't surrendered his dream years ago.

God puts dreams in our hearts to give us vision and inspiration and to guide us to the right path. That's why we have to make sure the dreams we have are not from our own flesh. The only way to be sure of that is to lay all of our dreams at His feet and let them die. And we must also die to them. The ones that are not from Him will be buried forever. The ones that *are* from Him will be given new life.

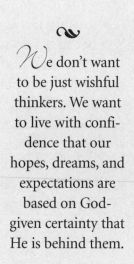

We don't want to be just wishful thinkers. We want to live with confidence that our hopes, dreams, and expectations are based on God-given certainty that He is behind them.

We don't want to be just wishful thinkers, always living in a dreamworld and never seeing anything of significance materialize. We don't want to be continually chasing after something God is not blessing. We want to live with confidence that our hopes, dreams, and expectations are based on God-given certainty that He is behind them. We want the hope that comes from God alone and is built on a foundation of His promises to us and His revealed purposes in us. This kind of hope is an anchor to the soul.

When my husband and I were first dating, I released Michael to the Lord every day. As much as I loved him, I did not want to manipulate a relationship to happen that was not meant to be. I had done that far too often in my past. I did it in my first marriage before I became a believer, and it ended in divorce less than two years later. As much as I wanted Michael, I desired what God had for me even more. Every day I sat at the feet of God and said, "Lord, I thank You that Michael is in my life. But if he is not the man You have to be my husband, I release him to You. Take him out of my life if we are not to be together. Close the door on this relationship if it is not of You. I'm walking step by step with You because I do not want to make another mistake."

When that door did not close, Michael and I were married and I knew it was God's will.

As the difficult times came in our marriage, I never wondered if God had really put us together. That issue had been settled long before when I fully surrendered the relationship to God. In the same year we celebrated our twenty-fifth wedding anniversary, my husband and I wrote a song called, "When the Dream Never Dies." One of the verses says,

> Isn't it just like the Lord to invite me
> To put all my dreams in His hands
> Forever releasing the grip that once held them
> Forever surrendering my plans

And then when He's certain it's not born of men
He calls for the fire to rekindle again
And asks me to know in my heart what's not
    seen with my eyes.
So the dream never dies.

Dying to our dreams is not fun. It's painful. Especially if our identity is wrapped up in them. But we have to do what God asks of us. And we must have a right attitude in the process or it's meaningless. The Bible says that if I "surrender my body to the flames, but have not love, I gain nothing" (1 Corinthians 13:3 NIV). Doing the right thing with a bad attitude does not work. Standing with our hands on our hips saying, "Okay, God, if you want to ruin me, go ahead," is not surrendering our dreams. It will definitely get God's attention, but it won't be the kind of attention we want.

The greatest breakthroughs in my life always came after a time of surrendering everything to God. I literally prostrated myself before Him with my face in the carpet and said, "God, I release everything to You and I freely give You permission to take out of my life what is not of You." I've done that with my children, my relatives, my friends, my work, my possessions, and my aspirations. It's difficult to say those words and mean them, but when we do the rewards are great.

Ask God if there are dreams in you that need to be laid down. If He says yes, this doesn't mean you have been doing anything wrong, or that you are out of the will of God. You

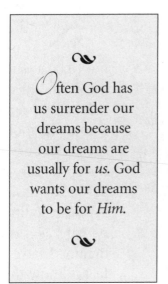

Often God has us surrender our dreams because our dreams are usually for *us.* God wants our dreams to be for *Him.*

might be right in the *center* of God's will. The dream you have may be the one God wants you to have. But often God has us surrender our dreams because our dreams usually are for *us*. We want to do something that feels good and right to *us*. God wants our dreams to be for *Him*. He wants us to do what we do for *His* glory.

Even if you are certain God has given you a vision or dream for your future, He will still ask you to surrender it to Him so thoroughly that you will think it's as good as dead.

God doesn't want any part of you to be unsurrendered, not even the dreams He has put in your heart. If you give Him *all* of your dreams, then you will see which ones are born of His Spirit. Pursuing the ones that aren't will only lead to misery, frustration, and unfulfillment. Dying to your dreams is difficult, but if you reach up and take your Heavenly Father's hand, He will shine His light on the situation and walk you through the process step by step.

Prayer Light

ord, I release all my hopes and dreams to You this day. If there is anything that I am longing for that is not to be a part of my life, I ask You to take away the desire for it so that what *should* be in my life will be released to me. I realize how dangerous it is to make idols of my dreams—to try and force my life to be what I have envisioned for myself. I lift up to You all that I desire, and I declare this day that I desire *You* more. I want the desires of my heart to line up with the desires of *Your* heart. As hard as it is for me to let go of the hopes and dreams I have for my life, I lay them all at Your feet. I know that as I die to them, You will either bury them forever or resurrect them to life. I accept Your decision and fully submit to it. Lead me in Your path, Lord. I don't want to speak a vision of my own heart (Jeremiah 23:16). You never said life would be easy. You said You would be with me. I now take each step with the light of Your presence as my guide.

Footlights

Where there is no vision, the people perish.

PROVERBS 29:18 (NIV)

This evil people, who refuse to hear My words,
who follow the dictates of their hearts, and walk
after other gods to serve them and worship them,
shall be just like this sash which is profitable
for nothing.

JEREMIAH 13:10

. . . if we hope for what we do not see,
we eagerly wait for it with perseverance.

ROMANS 8:25

Hear now My words:
If there is a prophet among you,
I, the LORD, make Myself known to him in
a vision; I speak to him in a dream.

NUMBERS 12:6

Beloved, now we are children of God; and it
has not yet been revealed what
we shall be, but we know that when
He is revealed, we shall be like Him,
for we shall see Him as He is.

1 JOHN 3:2

TWELVE

Waiting in the Wings

Has it ever seemed like you are waiting in the wings for the next scene of your life to start? The stage is dark and you're expecting the lights to go up and the curtain to rise. The first act may or may not have gone smoothly, but by now you've been on an extended intermission and you're beginning to wonder if the second act will ever begin.

How many times in our lives have we found ourselves waiting like that? Waiting for things to change. Waiting for something to happen. Waiting for life to get back to normal. Waiting for more time or more money. Waiting for the relationship to get better. Waiting for the right door to open. Waiting for the right person to come along. Waiting for somebody to notice. Waiting, waiting, waiting.

We don't like waiting. We want action. But God says waiting can be good, because that's how we learn patience. We respond that there's nothing wrong with patience, but we want it now!

We can't have patience, however, without the waiting. And God says we need patience because it will ultimately make us complete. That's because patience is one of the attributes of God. When we are patient, we are like Him. When we are being tested, walking in the wilderness, surrendering our dreams, or standing in the line of fire, part of what we are learning is to be patient.

I've found that it's best to view these waiting times by thinking of them as times of waiting on the Lord. Try it. You'll see. It's much easier to think about waiting on God than it is to be patient with your circumstances. Waiting on the Lord gives you the sense that something is going on—only you just can't see it. You are waiting in eager anticipation of what God is going to do next.

I remember shortly after I became a believer and surrendered my dreams to the Lord, I felt like my life was turned upside down and shaken and everything that wasn't supposed to be in it came flying out—including my acting career. As the doors to that dream closed, I went through a time of waiting. I certainly had not yet learned to welcome a waiting period as an opportunity to develop patience. I was used to fulfilling my own destiny. It took months of impatient misery before I finally said to God, "What do you want me to do, Lord?"

I clearly understood Him to say that I was to completely give up any thought of an acting career. Instead I was to wait on Him and write. From the time I was old enough to hold a pencil, I had written stories, poems, songs, articles, skits, and plays. It was something I just did—like breathing. But I wanted to perform, so people would love me and I wouldn't have to feel bad about myself. Acting was a dream I had for *me*. But once I laid it down, I knew I had heard from God.

As a step of faith I bought a desk. (Waiting doesn't mean doing nothing.) I had never owned a desk in my life, but I bought an antique rolltop and filled it full of writing supplies. I sat down each day with a pen and empty sheets of paper and waited on the Lord to tell me what I should write. I didn't have a specific assignment; I simply wrote. I wrote about what I knew, what I felt, what God was teaching me, what I hoped, what I dreamed, what I had lived, what I had learned, and what I observed. I was still waiting, only now I was writing about waiting.

It seemed like I was going to wait forever for that curtain to go up on the next scene of my life, but it was only a matter of months until the waiting period was over. Just like a violent thunderstorm that suddenly stops and the sun comes out, my waiting ended. Writing opportunities opened up to me, and I was set on a new path, walking step by step with God. That was eight books, sixty magazine articles, and hundreds of song lyrics ago. I've never looked back or missed what God took out of my life, nor did I regret the time of waiting.

Going through a waiting period doesn't mean there is nothing happening, because when you are waiting on the Lord, He is always moving in your life.

Even though it may not seem like it, as long as you are walking with the Lord you are going from "glory to glory" and "strength to strength." You are always going somewhere in God's plan. And His purpose for you is constantly being realized. But you have to be patient and wait for Him to accomplish it His way and in His time.

I performed in live theater for years. The dialogue and stage directions were set, so all of us in the cast would do the same thing over and over, night after night. Same costumes, same words, same props, same actions. It could have been a

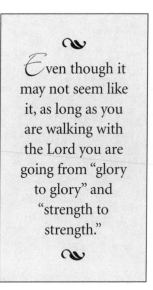

Even though it may not seem like it, as long as you are walking with the Lord you are going from "glory to glory" and "strength to strength."

boring experience where we ended up just going through the motions waiting for the play to be over. But we didn't, for one good reason. The audience was different every time. We performed it for new ears and new eyes each night, and that kept the play fresh for us as well.

If you ever feel like you are just going through the motions in your own life, don't let yourself become frustrated over it. Know that God's mercies to you are new every morning and as a result, God freshly hears your words spoken to Him as well. There is no such thing as the same old prayer. Each prayer you pray, even if it's about the same thing, has new life to it every time you pray it. Every day you have another opportunity to affect your future with the words you speak to God. Even though you may not see results as soon as you would like, much is happening in the spirit realm that you don't see. Each prayer sets something in motion.

Besides praying, there are other things you can do to keep your season of waiting on the Lord from turning into a dark time. Stay in God's Word and keep learning about Him. Ask the Lord to show you the talents and abilities He has given you and how you should develop them. Ask Him to reveal anything you need to start or stop doing. Perhaps He is waiting on *you*.

If you continue to walk with God and take the steps you know are right, you will get where you need to go. It may seem like forever, but don't be discouraged. God has been known to do a quick work for which He has been preparing a long time. Let Him sustain you in the interim. Tell yourself that you will "Rest in the LORD, and wait patiently for Him . . ." (Psalm 37:7).

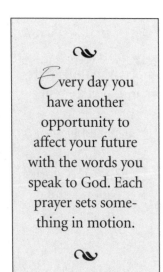

∿

*E*very day you have another opportunity to affect your future with the words you speak to God. Each prayer sets something in motion.

∿

Patience is not resignation. It's joyful anticipation of the glory that is before you. Actors use that time before the curtain goes up to get focused and prepare for what's ahead. As you wait for the next scene of your life to begin, center yourself in the Lord, tell Him you are content to wait for His perfect timing, and ask Him to keep you from stumbling into any bad lighting.

Prayer Light

*L*ord, I wait upon You this day. I put my hope in Your Word and ask that You would fill me afresh with Your Holy Spirit and wash away all anxiety or doubt. Shine Your spotlight into any dark corner of my soul that needs to be exposed. I don't want my impatience or lack of trust to stand in the way of all You desire to do in me. I realize that even when my life seems to be standing still, as long as I cling to You I am moving forward on the path You have for me. As I wait on You, help me to grow in my understanding of Your ways, and not succumb to impatience or discouragement because my timetable does not coincide with Yours. Strengthen my faith to depend on Your perfect timing for my life. Help me to rest in You and be content with the step I'm on and the light You have given me.

Footlights

. . . those who wait on the LORD
Shall renew their strength;
They shall mount up with wings like eagles,
They shall run and not be weary,
They shall walk and not faint.

ISAIAH 40:31

I wait for the LORD, my soul waits,
And in His Word I do hope.
My soul waits for the LORD
More than those who watch for the morning.

PSALM 130:5-6

Count it all joy when you fall into various trials,
knowing that the testing of your faith produces
patience. But let patience have its perfect work,
that you may be perfect and complete,
lacking nothing.

JAMES 1:2-4

The LORD is good to those who wait for Him,
To the soul who seeks Him.
It is good that one should
hope and wait quietly
For the salvation of the LORD.

LAMENTATIONS 3:25-26

Wait on the LORD;
Be of good courage,
And He shall strengthen
your heart.

PSALM 27:14

THIRTEEN

Expecting a Call

God has a great purpose for each one of us. There is a call from God on your life and mine. The question is, will we listen to find out what it is?

We can be in the dark about the call of God on our lives for two reasons: either we have not heard God's call and we're living as though we have, or we have heard God's call and we're living as though we have not.

I've seen many people who were too busy, too drugged out, too tired, too preoccupied, or too in pursuit of riches and fame to hear God calling them. Others were afraid they might be called to insignificance and so they didn't want to know about it. I've known others still who clearly heard the call of God and ran away from it. The direct line from heaven was ringing and they turned up the volume on their lives so they wouldn't have to hear God and answer. I've also known people with such a low opinion of themselves that they didn't believe God had them destined for anything great. So when the call came, they thought it must be for somebody else and didn't respond.

The only reason it appears that some people are "more called" by God than others is that they were expecting the call and answered it.

In the early days of telephones, people had party lines. Several households were on the same phone line and anyone in any of those households could pick up the phone and listen in on your conversation. This meant that by afternoon there might be many different opinions and interpretations of the conversation you had that morning. Receiving God's call does not happen that way. God's line to you is not a party line. You won't hear conflicting opinions. His call is entirely personal and private, and He will speak directly to you.

I'm not saying that God won't speak to someone else about you as well, because confirmation of His call is important. But true confirmation will only come from a person with a direct line to God themselves, who seeks to know God's will on your behalf. It will be someone with God-given authority in your life such as a parent, pastor, counselor, or mentor. But it won't be that only *they* hear and you don't. And do not ever think that you have strayed so far away from God that you've forever missed your call.

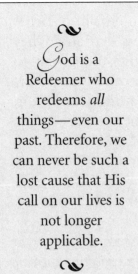

*G*od is a Redeemer who redeems *all* things—even our past. Therefore, we can never be such a lost cause that His call on our lives is not longer applicable.

God will find you wherever you are. You can never be in so remote a place that He cannot bring you into all He has planned for you.

It never entered my mind that I had a life's calling until I was in my early thirties, and then I thought about it with deep regret. I was certain that by this late in life, I had passed up any opportunities for God to do something significant through me. Having lived far away from Him for so long, I despaired over what I considered an unredeemable loss. It wasn't until I understood that

God is a Redeemer who redeems *all* things—even our past—that I began to have hope. The Bible says that "the gifts and the calling of God are irrevocable" (Romans 11:29). When God issues a call, He doesn't take it back. He only waits for us to move into it. Therefore, we can never be such a lost cause that His call on our lives is no longer applicable.

Everyone shares certain calls on their life. For example, we are all called to partake of His divine nature (2 Peter 1:3-4), we are called to His eternal glory (1 Peter 5:10), and we are called to bless others (1 Peter 3:9). But we are individually called according to His own purpose. In other words, He has a specific calling for each one of us.

Many people know their calling, but can't see how it will ever be realized in the details of their lives. That's because they are trying to accomplish it in their own strength. But God doesn't say, "Here's what I want you to do with your life, now go do it." He first gives a vision and then says, "Walk step by step with Me and *I'll* do it through you."

Also, the whole of our call does not suddenly drop in our laps. We grow into it a step at a time, and it is realized gradually. For example, I know that I'm called to help people who are hurting, discouraged, or unfulfilled find a way out of their pain and frustration and see Jesus as the answer for every area of their lives. But I didn't just start doing that one day.

First, I asked God what I was to do with my life. Then when I began to hear, I didn't understand exactly what it was I was hearing. I had to surrender my dreams and watch the doors to what I thought was opportunity close. During the quietness of the waiting period that followed, I felt a tug on my heart that I would never have otherwise noticed in the noisy fast lane where I had been traveling. I sensed what

God wanted me to do, but I still didn't see how it could ever come about. I knew there was no way I could make it happen on my own.

Having a sense of God's call on my life forced me to declare my complete dependence upon Him more fervently than ever before. I was convinced that the only way anything of lasting significance would ever happen through me was if He accomplished it. As I waited for Him to do that, there were times I doubted whether I had even heard Him correctly. But eventually doors opened and as I walked through them the Lord blessed the outcome. When opportunities came my way that were not in line with my calling, I knew it. In certain moments of insecurity, I did accept a couple of offers that were outside of what I understood to be God's purpose for my life. The results brought emptiness, and I knew I was doing something that fell far below what God had called me to do.

If you feel called to something better than what you are doing now, let me assure you that it is probably because you are. If you have never sought God about His plans and purposes for your life, do that now. If you have already done that, then there must be a purpose for what you are doing at this moment that you cannot see. Or perhaps you have unsurrendered dreams. In any case, know that He will not leave you where you are forever.

This doesn't mean you have to accept everything that comes your way as the will of God. Far from it. Ask Him about it. Say, "Lord, is what I am doing consistent with Your purpose in my life? If it is Your will, I submit to it and embrace You in it. If it isn't, then make me what You created me to be." As long as you are consistently praying about it, God will either take you where you're supposed to be, or give you grace to remain where you are until He says it's time to move on.

Keep in mind that once you hear God's call on your life, it doesn't mean that things will start happening immediately. You will most likely experience a time of waiting until He decides you are ready. So don't let the waiting period turn into a dark time that causes you to doubt whether you've heard God at all. Keep in mind that in this time He wants you to forget any plans you might have for accomplishing your purpose on your own. He wants you to be totally convinced it won't happen without Him.

God's call on all of us is to be a light to those who are in darkness, but sometimes He has to take us through our own darkness so we will learn to depend totally on His light.

Oswald Chambers said, "If I am going to approach the holy ground, I must get into the right frame of mind—the excellency of a broken heart."[1] Our hearts break when we think we have missed our destiny. We suffer over unfulfilled purpose. But God perfects our hearts when we suffer. He makes us humble and compassionate, and these are two traits we must have for success in the call He has for us.

Don't be afraid of the perfecting process that prepares you to move into God's call on your life. It will establish, strengthen, and settle you (1 Peter 5:10). Just stand strong through the fire and you will be purified, molded, humbled, and made ready for what He has for you to do. If you walk step by step with God, you'll come out of that time with a sense of His presence and power that will make it all worthwhile. It will set you on the path to greatness.

❧

*T*oo often when people think of greatness, it stirs up images in their minds of having great talent, riches, fame, or accomplishments. But greatness is not about *us;* it's about *His* greatness *in* us.

❧

Let me clarify the meaning of greatness. Too often when people think of greatness, it stirs up images in their minds of having great talent, great riches, great fame, great influence, great power, or great accomplishments. They mistakenly believe that greatness comes about because of something they are or something they have. But greatness is not about *us*; it's about *His* greatness *in* us.

God's idea of greatness is having a heart, soul, and spirit so full of His greatness that it manifests through us.

In the Bible, the word "great" is nearly always used to describe who God is: "For the LORD is great and greatly to be praised . . ." (1 Chronicles 16:25). Or what God has done: "The LORD has done great things for us, and we are glad" (Psalm 126:3). A great person is one who obeys God: "Whoever therefore breaks one of the least of these commandments, and teaches men so, shall be called least in the kingdom of heaven; but whoever does and teaches them, he shall be called great in the kingdom of heaven" (Matthew 5:19). A great person is one who is a servant: "Yet it shall not be so among you; but whoever desires to become great among you, let him be your servant" (Matthew 20:26).

When we acknowledge God's greatness through our worship of Him, we invite His greatness to dwell *in* us. When we obey God and serve Him, then He does great things *through* us. This is the kind of greatness God has called us to in our lives.

If you heard God's call to greatness years ago and have been following it faithfully, that doesn't mean you won't hear a fresh, new call now. Or maybe God will newly define the old one. Whichever it is, you need ears to hear. If your heart is not quickened with anticipation over what God is going to do through you, perhaps your listening has become dulled by the processes of life. Find time to get away with the Lord and let Him speak to you again.

Remember that in order to hear God's call, you must be expecting a call. You need faith that He *will* speak to you, that you *can* hear Him, and that it *will* be good news. Say, "I have set the Lord always before me" (Psalm 16:8), and expect to hear His voice. When an encounter with the living God is your greatest desire, you can be sure you will have it.

If you have not heard anything from God, may I politely suggest that there *is* a person-to-person call on line one for you. You'd better take it. It's God wanting to cast a definitive light on your path.

Prayer Light

Lord, I know You have great purpose for me and a plan for my life. Open my ears to hear Your voice leading me into all You have for me. Align my heart with Yours and prepare me to understand where You would have me to go and what You would have me to do. Help me to hear Your call. If my expectations and plans are out of alignment with Your will for me, I surrender them to You. I let my desires for myself die. I would rather endure the suffering of that than the pain of never realizing what You made me to be. Because I want to hear Your voice say, "Well done, my good and faithful servant," when I meet You face to face, I will listen for Your voice now. I don't want to be unfruitful and unfulfilled because I never clearly heard Your call. I want You to fill me with Your greatness so that I may do great things for others as You have called me to do. I commit to walking this road step by step with You so that I may fully become all that You have made me to be.

Footlights

... you are a chosen generation, a royal priesthood,
a holy nation, His own special people, that you
may proclaim the praises of Him who called you
out of darkness into His marvelous light. ...

1 PETER 2:9

... whom He predestined, these He also called;
whom He called, these He also justified; and whom
He justified, these He also glorified.

ROMANS 8:30

... the God of our Lord Jesus Christ, the Father of
glory, may give to you the spirit of wisdom and
revelation in the knowledge of Him, the eyes of
your understanding being enlightened;
that you may know what is the hope of His calling,
what are the riches of the glory of His inheritance in
the saints, and what is the exceeding greatness of His
power toward us who believe, according to the
working of His mighty power. ...

EPHESIANS 1:17-19

"You are the light of the world.
A city that is set on a hill cannot be hidden.
... Let your light so shine before men,
that they may see your good works
and glorify your Father in heaven."

MATTHEW 5:14,16

FOURTEEN

Believing It's Not Over till It's Over

You might be too young to appreciate this now, but there may come a time in your life when it feels like you have outlived your usefulness and purpose. You fear that God and everyone else is through with you and you're no longer relevant. You start to believe that although you may have *had* a call on your life, it's over now. You're being put out to pasture.

The enemy of your soul wants you to believe that you have no purpose so that you can actually become all those things you fear becoming. It's one of his most common deceptions. But the truth is, God is *never* through with you. He *always* has a plan for your life. There is no time limit on His call or what He wants to do in and through you. God will use you for His purposes until the day you go to be with Him. And don't let yourself be convinced otherwise.

What *may* be true about what you are experiencing is that life as you have known it is changing. What existed *before* may be over, but what is *ahead* for you is as great or perhaps much greater. Just when you suspect things may be winding down in your life, God will do something new. He may call you to rework the details of your present walk, or He might set you out on a completely new path. God will call you to a new time, a new assignment, and a new work of His grace. That is, of course, if you are open to letting Him do what He wants. This is where staying attentive to His leading and being willing to move accordingly is important.

I know a man who owned a successful business for years. In his late fifties, he experienced some health problems that forced him to retire. At first He was discouraged and thought his life was over. But he and his wife began to sense a leading from God to move to a more favorable climate and adopt a less stressful lifestyle in order to develop a successful ministry to troubled or runaway teenage girls. It was a service they had always enjoyed volunteering part-time for at their church, but now they were able to devote themselves to it full-time. They are presently more fulfilled than they have ever been.

We are such creatures of habit and so resistant to change that God sometimes has to shut off the way things were in our lives so He can bring us into the way He wants us to be.

When my husband and I made our move from California to Tennessee the transition was very difficult physically, mentally, and emotionally. Moving is upsetting anyway, but relocating from one part of the country that was so completely different from the other at age fifty was too much, and I let God know it.

"Lord, don't you realize we're too old for this? We don't have it in us to

God will call you to a new time, a new assignment, and a new work of His grace. That is, of course, if you are open to letting Him do what He wants.

start all over again. It's too hard. Are you putting us out to pasture?"

We knew that we had followed the leading of the Lord, but it wasn't until our California home was destroyed in the Northridge earthquake a few months after we moved that we stopped questioning Him. That was answer enough. We were certain we had made the right decision. We even knew why we had never been able to sell the house. Anyone living in it surely would have been seriously injured or even killed.

Over the years that we've been here, many opportunities and blessings for Michael and me and each of our children have come along that would not have been available to us had we stayed in California. What originally seemed like the end became a new beginning. But new beginnings don't happen without something ending.

Major life changes can be scary. But if we don't cling desperately to the old life, the new experiences can be exciting as well. Trying to keep things from changing only makes the process miserable. It's far less upsetting to just let the old go and walk step by step with God into the new life He has for us.

Many of the greatest people of the Bible achieved their most significant accomplishments in their later years, at a time when they thought their productivity was coming to a close. Noah was a very old man when God called him to build the ark. "Noah was six hundred years old when the floodwaters were on the earth" (Genesis 7:6). If people can live to be ninety years old today, Noah was the equivalent of a sixty-year-old man when he and his family gave up life as they had always known it and got on board the ark. His experience was not that of a young man dreaming a young man's dream. Noah was definitely beyond the time of midlife crisis when God called him to do his greatest work.

Even Moses, just before He led the Israelites out of Egypt, thought his life was over in terms of ever doing anything significant for the Lord. Though he always had a passion in his heart to free his people from their enslavement—which was God's call on his life—it only made matters worse when he tried to help them *his* way. It was not until he had been thoroughly pruned, seasoned, literally put out to pasture, and trained to follow the Lord step by step that God used him powerfully.

Abraham was one hundred years old and his wife, Sarah, was ninety when God touched their lives and she finally became pregnant and gave birth to their first child. They thought they were too old for that to ever happen, but God was just beginning a new time in their lives. It fulfilled God's call on them and it affected the entire world and all of history.

I wonder where would we be if Noah, Moses, Abraham, Sarah, or any of the other great men and women of the Bible had listened to the voice that said, "You're too old to do anything significant." What if Noah had responded to God by saying, "Me? Build a boat? I'm too over the hill." Or if Moses had insisted, "Pharaoh is never going to listen to an old geezer like me." Or if Abraham and Sarah had looked at each other and said, "Forget it." None of us would even be here had they not seen a vision of what God had for their future and allowed Him to walk them step by step into a new time in their lives.

> ∾
>
> *G*od may call you and me to do our greatest work in our fifties, sixties, seventies, or even eighties and beyond. What a wonderful thing to look forward to!
>
> ∾

God may call you and me to do our greatest work in our fifties, sixties, seventies, or even eighties and beyond. What a wonderful thing to look forward to! God does not devalue people over a certain age like society does. Big business may tell a man in his fifties or sixties that he is too old to do the work he has done all his life. Or that he cannot be hired because of his advanced age, even though he may be every bit as capable as someone younger. But God does not put a lifetime of experience and knowledge into you and then put you out to pasture. Your life is never over until it's over. And that's when God calls you home to be with Him.

If the job you've been doing ends, or the provision you've known shuts off, or the fulfillment level of your work and activities ceases, or something major happens to change the status of your life, don't be alarmed. These could be signs of a change God is doing in your life. He may be getting you ready to enter into a new and exciting season. God's Word says that those who love Him and live His way will bear fruit into old age and always be fresh and flourishing.

If life as you have known it and the path that you have walked seem to be ending, draw especially close to God and He will reveal what your next step is to be.

Although God has promised we will bear fruit into old age, remember that fruit is seasonal. We won't necessarily bear fruit constantly. We will have seasons of rest so the soil of our lives won't be depleted. When God wants to produce a fresh new crop through you, don't strive against what is intended to be a time of plowing up and preparing the soil. It doesn't mean you are going to wither. God promises that you will be filled with living water, bring forth new life, and prosper in all you do. Trust Him. He has never been closer. Become more dependent upon the Lord than ever. Lose yourself completely in Him so that He becomes everything. Follow Him so closely that you will not miss the harvest He has for you.

No matter what age you are, God has a path for you. It will undoubtedly take you someplace you've not been before.

Be willing to let Him prepare you as He sees fit. Follow the leading of the Lord as you place your hand in His, and trust that the light that is in you can never be put out.

───────── *Prayer Light* ─────────

*L*ord, thank You that my life is never over here on this earth until You say it is. And when that time comes, I will see You face to face and dwell in Your presence. Thank You that You never give up on me, even when I have given up on myself. I am so happy that no matter what age I am, I will always have purpose because You have great things for me to do. When it's time for me to do something different, help me not to cling to the past or be afraid to move into the future You have for me. My times are in Your hands, and I know that I am secure as long as I can walk through them all with You. Give me strength, courage, health, wisdom, revelation, and faith for the journey. I trust You to keep me on the right path and to continue giving me the light I need for the step I'm on.

Footlights

Those who are planted in the house of the LORD
Shall flourish in the courts of our God.
They shall still bear fruit in old age;
They shall be fresh and flourishing.

PSALM 92:13-14

Listen to counsel and receive instruction,
That you may be wise in your latter days.

PROVERBS 19:20

Even to your old age, I am He,
And even to gray hairs I will carry you!
I have made, and I will bear;
Even I will carry, and will deliver you.

ISAIAH 46:4

You will show me the path of life;
In Your presence is fullness of joy;
At Your right hand are pleasures forevermore.

PSALM 16:11

. . . when I am old and gray-headed,
O God, do not forsake me,
Until I declare Your strength to this generation,
Your power to everyone who is to come.

PSALM 71:18

FIFTEEN

Surviving Disappointment

Disappointment is inevitable. That's because life can never consistently live up to our expectations.

When my friend Marcie's husband chose another woman to be with instead of her, the disappointment she felt was engulfing. She could have turned to alcohol, bitterness, revenge, or another man's arms, but she turned instead to the Comforter. She drew closer to the Lord and let Him provide relief from her complex feelings of guilt, resentment, failure, and depression. She relied on His unfailing love and steady hand through the dark times of struggle as she carved out a new life for herself and her children. She declined to sit in the darkness of unforgiveness, but instead walked a step at a time in the light of the Lord. She refused to allow her disappointment with the way things turned out to shadow her life for years to come. Eventually she was able to find happiness again.

Life certainly doesn't always turn out the way we imagine it will. When it doesn't, how can we survive the disappointment? How can we get through those dark times?

Often our greatest times of disappointment come when someone fails us, or we at least *feel* that they have. People can hurt us deeply. Sometimes they know what they are doing, while other times they're only doing the best they know how to do with the tools they have. In either case, the level of fulfillment and happiness we experience in our lives doesn't depend on other people; it depends on God. Of course, we do rely on other people for certain things, and it's painful when they let us down. But the ultimate success or joy of our life should not depend on them. We don't have to prolong suffering over what others do or don't do to us, because ultimately our reward is in God's hands.

It's also seriously disappointing when we believe *we* have failed in some way, perhaps due to our own carelessness or in spite of our best efforts. Or we *think* we have failed when we really haven't at all. And we sit in darkness over it, torturing ourselves. The regret and condemnation pounds us down like a giant sledgehammer to our soul. "If only I hadn't . . ." "If I just would have . . ." "Why didn't I . . ." It's a weight we can't carry and were never meant to.

How wonderful it is to know that even in a darkness of our own creation, God is still there and so is His light.

Even when we have to bear the consequences for the wrong choices we've made, God is still on our side. "When I fall, I will arise; when I sit in darkness, the LORD will be a light to me" (Micah 7:8). How wonderful it is to know that even in a darkness of our own creation, God is still there and so is His light. I think that's what makes us love Him most. His grace. We realize how little we deserve it and how far short of His glory we fall, yet He loves and accepts us anyway. Even in our greatest depth of failure, God brings good out of it as long as we reach humbly to Him.

We make a mistake in expecting too much from ourselves, other people, and life, when our expectations should be from God.

One time my husband was very disappointed about a big work project that fell through. Someone had promised something great that did not materialize, and the result seemed to be financial as well as personal devastation. Not being one to look on the bright side, he was very upset about it.

"This project isn't more important than God's will, is it?" I asked him.

He hesitated a little too long for my comfort, then gave a begrudging and controlled, "No."

"Then how do you know God doesn't have something far better for you?" I asked.

He gave me a look that can only be described as equal parts hope, doubt, and suppressed irritation all rolled into one facial expression. "I don't," he replied.

"Don't waste your time being upset," I encouraged him. "This is probably more of an opportunity than a disaster, and we should thank God for it."

He still was not cheered.

It seemed like a long time, but it was actually only a few weeks later that he was offered a project far greater in every respect than the one which had been cancelled. There was no way he could have done both, and he would have had to turn the better one down if he'd already been involved in the first project.

God often allows hard things to happen in our lives in order to bless us in some way. If we are willing to allow for that possibility in everything that happens, it saves us from being devastated by people and situations that are ultimately going to be used for God's glory. If we surrender our disappointment to God and say, "Be my light and lead me through this, Lord," His work will be accomplished faster. But if we wallow in the darkness of bitterness, casting blame upon God and other people, we end up suffering more.

When Moses brought the Israelites out of slavery in Egypt, they had to choose to walk God's way. In their bondage under Pharaoh, they didn't have to make choices; they only had to do what they were told. Instead of choosing to see God's hand in the moment, they blamed Moses and God for everything that disappointed them. As a result, their suffering was prolonged.

Oswald Chambers says, "The agony of a man's affliction is often necessary to put him into the right mood to face the fundamental things of life."[1]

When disappointing things happen to you, ask God to help you discern His truth about what you are experiencing. Ask *Him* to reign in the situation instead of your feelings. It's easy to go with anger or hurt, but far more rewarding to find God's blessing in the situation instead.

> If you will maintain a humble, submitted, faith-filled, expectant heart, you will see God's goodness manifest in the midst of all that's happening to you.

It pleases God when you have faith enough in the midst of your disappointment to put your hope and expectations in Him.

When you experience disappointment, do not run into the arms of bitterness or unforgiveness. Run to your Father's arms instead so He can hold and sustain you. If you will maintain a humble, submitted, faith-filled, expectant heart, you will see God's goodness manifest in the midst of all that's happening to you. He will use this experience to bring you closer to Him, and your greatest treasure will be a deep sense of His presence. He will make things right, and He is the only one who can. Remember that no matter how dark times of disappointment become, God is still your light. Walk in the light He gives you.

Prayer Light

Lord, You alone are my guide, my companion, my strength, and my life. I need no other to fulfill my expectations, for all my hopes and expectations are in You. In times of great disappointment, I will cling to You. I will walk through them with You. Show me what You want me to see. Teach me what You want me to learn. Reveal Your truth to me. I refuse to allow disappointment to color my mind and emotions and outlook. I put You in charge of every detail of my life, even the pain I feel in my heart. Use it to perfect me and bring glory to You. Thank You for Your endless goodness toward me. You supply all my needs. I lift my hands to You, and I trust that the light I have is sufficient for what I face this day and this moment.

Footlights

My soul, wait silently for God alone,
For my expectation is from Him.

Psalm 62:5

They cried to you and were saved;
in you they trusted and were not disappointed.

PSALM 22:5 (NIV)

Now hope does not disappoint, because the
love of God has been poured out in our hearts
by the Holy Spirit who was given to us.

ROMANS 5:5

. . . judge nothing before the time, until the Lord
comes, who will both bring to light the hidden
things of darkness and reveal the counsels
of the hearts. Then each one's praise
will come from God.

1 CORINTHIANS 4:5

The LORD will perfect that which concerns me. . . .

PSALM 138:8

SIXTEEN

Traveling Through the Dark Moments of Relationships

Relationships can be difficult to navigate because of one major variable—*the other person!* Due to that great unknown, we may be going along doing the best we know how and all of a sudden find ourselves in the middle of a relationship crisis. Our darkest hours can come because of the troubled times we have with people.

Any kind of relationship can bring pain. Strife with a mother or father, a brother or sister, a husband or wife, a son or daughter, a relative, friend, pastor, boss, neighbor, boyfriend, girlfriend, or coworker can cause us to experience a knot in our stomach, a lump in our throat, and a loss of sleep. That's because whether we want to acknowledge it or not, relationships are very important to each of us. We can't live without them. Nor were we ever intended to. God never planned for us to live entirely separate from other people.

Much of what God wants to work in us will come about as we grow in our relationships with the people God puts in our lives.

The enemy of our soul does not want our relationships to work. He knows that as our relationships are destroyed, so too will be our strength and effectiveness. After all, how effective can we be when our marriages fall apart, we're estranged from our children, we fight with our siblings, we don't get along with our coworkers, or we have no strong friendships? If we can be convinced that these relationships are not worth the effort it takes to fight for them, then the enemy has us in darkness. Right where he wants us.

In one of the many prayer groups I have had over the past twenty years, a situation arose that I knew could easily divide the group. It would certainly have split us down the middle, with each person taking one side or the other. During one of the dark nights of my travail over the situation, I prayed, "Lord, each one of these women is far more important to me than this issue that has the potential to divide us. I know that each one sees this matter from her own perspective and believes she is right. I don't even know how to pray about this because I see it from my own perspective and I feel *I* see it right. But I am willing to let go of *my* perspective and *my* desire to be right, so that *Your* Spirit of peace will prevail. I see where this could possibly be heading and I pray that Your Spirit of unity would reign in each of us and shine light on our path. I refuse to allow the enemy to bring strife and destruction. Let there be no severing of friendships or wounding of hearts."

I released the situation into God's hands and watched His work as He walked me one step at a time through it. Over the next several

> ⮜
> The enemy of our soul does not want our relationships to work. He knows that as our relationships are destroyed, so too will be our strength and effectiveness.
> ⮜

weeks He powerfully transformed the entire matter and it dissipated. The love and commitment each woman had toward God and each other became the focus and made the issue at hand pale to nothing, eventually becoming a non-issue. Had any one of us insisted that we were right, the outcome would have been quite different.

Every relationship requires a sacrifice. Every sacrifice has a reward. If we knew the rewards, we wouldn't hesitate to make the sacrifices. Part of the sacrifice we must pay in a relationship is laying down our pride and our needs. We need to be loved, cared for, valued, and respected, but we never get those needs met when we demand them. We get them met when we give them up.

Humbling ourselves and putting the other person's needs before our own can resurrect a relationship that has suffered mortal wounds.

Marriage, especially, has the greatest potential for deep emotional injury and by far the stiffest requirements for sacrifice. That's because the person who knows us best can hurt us most. If that weren't so, we would not see such a high divorce rate. It takes too much effort to dissolve a marriage, divide up everything, and establish separate living quarters. Even more so if children are involved. No one does it lightly. No one comes out unscathed. Yet millions of people get divorced because their hurt is so great that they believe staying in the marriage will destroy them.

I do not condemn nor criticize anyone who has chosen the path of divorce. I chose it myself at one time. I was married before I became a believer, and my first marriage did not last two years. But for me it was two years of disaster, and I believed I would die if I stayed in it. When I married again, it was under very different circumstances. Both my husband and I were committed to God and to living His way. Over the past twenty-five years of marriage we have tried to relate to one another the way God designed us to, but it has not always been easy. We experienced dark times in our marriage when the selfishness of our flesh almost brought us to the brink of collapse.

On one particularly dark night of discord, I remember going before God and saying, "Lord, I can't endure the pain I feel in this marriage another day. If You don't intervene, it's over."

The Lord, without judgement, answered the cries of my heart, saying, "If you will lay down your life for My sake and reach up your hand to Me, I will guide you through these rough waters and you *will* get to the other side of this storm and walk on calmer seas than ever before."

God did not promise that my husband would ever change or that things would be any different than they were right then, but He did promise that He would go through the storm with me. He would sustain me and my greatest blessing would come from Him. But first I had to lay down my life in prayer for my husband like I had never done before. I had to give up my desire to see my needs met, and instead pray for God to work in my husband and meet *his* needs. It was a very difficult lesson to learn, but as I walked with God through those dark moments and made the sacrifice He asked me to make, I saw His resurrecting power bring life and restoration to our marriage.

Let me make one thing clear. Laying down your life for a relationship does not mean allowing someone to physically or emotionally destroy you. Abuse does *not* get better on its own. The abuser has a serious problem that must be resolved, and you are keeping that person in bondage when you permit him to continue to abuse you. It cannot lead to life for either of you. Nothing of redemption comes out of it—only bitterness and the destruction of the soul.

God has far more for you than that. Don't allow any abuse to continue!

Problems in any marriage require a special portion of God's grace and revelation for each moment. We must ask God every day to take all our hopes, expectations, dreams, and disappointments, and give us more of His love, patience, kindness, and a willingness to sacrifice. I stayed in my marriage and saw God work miraculous change, and it is better now than it has ever been. But the good did not come without my sacrifice of laying down what *I* wanted and doing what *God* wanted.

A relational crisis with our children is right next to marital strife on the misery scale. When a relationship with a child breaks down, our heart breaks as well. But when we walk step by step with God through each crisis, we will see Him do a miraculous work of transforming, restoring, and healing. When we bring God into the midst of the situation, everyone benefits.

The most difficult confrontations my husband and I have had with our children, as upsetting as they were at the time, have brought about the greatest growth and deliverance in both their lives and ours. Each instance bonded us closer together. As we prayed through many a painfully dark night for them, strongholds of the enemy that were seeking to encroach upon their lives were revealed and broken down. We stood in the line of fire, refused to be afraid of the dark, surrendered our dreams for them, survived disappointment, held on to the light God gave us, and waited for Him to move.

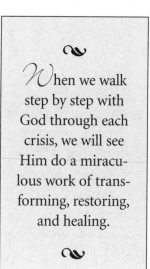

When we walk step by step with God through each crisis, we will see Him do a miraculous work of transforming, restoring, and healing.

Staying on the right path in *any* relationship means getting rid of excess baggage that keeps us from seeing the light. Unforgiveness and jealousy are examples of such baggage. These negative attitudes will drive a wedge into any relationship. And they are always evident to other people, even if they don't recognize exactly what it is they are observing. The dark moments of relationships can be kept to a minimum if we humble ourselves before God and ask Him to walk us step by step through every layer of unforgiveness and jealousy. It's a sacrifice that always brings a great reward.

The best way to protect all of your relationships is to make sure your primary relationship is with the Lord. Then commit each of your relationships to God and ask Him to be Lord over all of them. Cover them in prayer and seek God's hand of reconciliation where it needs to happen. Even though we can do a great deal to offer our love and forgiveness to other people, only God can soften their hearts enough for them to receive it. Ask Him to do that, too.

If you are having trouble with a particular person who is causing you to feel so much pain that it incapacitates you, release him or her to God and allow the Lord to take the relationship away if He so chooses. He may need to do that for just a season if something needs to be worked in each of you individually that can't happen when you are together. Or there may exist some unhealthy aspect of the relationship that He wants to make right. Perhaps you are unequally yoked. After all, "what communion has light with darkness?" (2 Corinthians 6:14). If that relationship is to be restored again, *He* will restore it on *His* terms. If not, you can trust that it was not meant to be a part of your life. If that person is never to have the place in your life that you want him or her to have, don't try to hang on and make it happen. Relationships only work when the Lord is in charge of them.

In ironing out the wrinkles in relationships, I find it's best to remember two things—release people and cling to God. Gaining that perspective can help you rise above the failings of flesh and elevate you to the realm of the miraculous. The stronger your relationship is with the Lord, the better your other relationships will be. The dark moments of any relationship can strengthen your walk with the Lord as you draw closer to Him. So make Him the focus of your attention, and trust Him to shine a special light at the crossroads of where your path intersects with the path of another person.

———————— *Prayer Light* ————————

*L*ord, I give all my relationships to You and ask that You be in charge of them. May Your spirit of unity reign in each one. If any are not of You, take them out of my life. Concerning my relationship with (_____), I ask that Your spirit of love and peace would reign between us. I relinquish my hold and release him (her) to You. Lead him (her) in the way You would have him (her) to go. Bless him (her) and help him (her) to have a closer walk with You. Guide us both through any difficult times and help us to discern clearly the hand of the enemy when he comes to lie and destroy.

Shine Your light of revelation into every relationship I have and show me Your truth. Illuminate any darkness of unforgiveness in me and I will confess it to You as sin. Bring reconciliation and clarity in place of misunderstanding.

Where I need to humbly extend myself, enable me to make any necessary sacrifice and not cater to the cries of my flesh. Help me to lay down my life in prayer for my family, friends, and others You have put in my life. Teach me how to love the way that You do. I join my hand in Yours as I travel the path of relationships with Your unconditional love as my guiding light.

Footlights

He who says he is in the light, and hates his brother,
is in darkness until now.

1 JOHN 2:9

If we say that we have fellowship with Him,
and walk in darkness, we lie and do not
practice the truth. But if we walk in the
light as He is in the light, we have
fellowship with one another, and
the blood of Jesus Christ His
Son cleanses us from all sin.

1 JOHN 1:6-7

Let nothing be done through selfish
ambition or conceit, but in lowliness of mind
let each esteem others better than himself. Let each of
you look out not only for his own interests,
but also for the interests of others.

PHILIPPIANS 2:3-4

Let all bitterness, wrath, anger, clamor, and evil
speaking be put away from you, with all malice.
And be kind to one another, tenderhearted,
forgiving one another, even as
God in Christ forgave you.

EPHESIANS 4:31-32

"Greater love has no one than this,
than to lay down one's life for his friends."

JOHN 15:13

SEVENTEEN

Walking in the Midst of the Overwhelming

At some point in each of our lives, we may find our world being violently shaken. Such traumatic experiences as a devastating illness, a debilitating accident, desertion by a spouse, the death of a loved one, criminal violence, financial ruin, or a natural disaster can occur with disarming suddenness. How can we be prepared to stand strong in the midst of overwhelming circumstances that come without warning?

Let me give you an example of an overwhelming circumstance. It's suddenly being awakened out of a deep sleep, in the thick, black darkness of night, to the deafening roar and violent shaking of a severe earthquake. I endured too many earthquakes like this in Los Angeles during the forty years that I lived there, and they were by far the most traumatic experiences of my life. I *never* got used to them.

Before I started walking with the Lord, each earthquake produced heart-stopping terror in me. After coming into a personal relationship with God, I still experienced the terror, but then came a reassuring sense of God's presence. I knew He was there in the midst of it.

I remember one particularly strong earthquake that happened when I was living alone in a first-floor apartment of a three-story building. This is an especially dangerous place to be because in older apartment buildings constructed before certain codes were established, the higher floors can easily crash down upon the lowest one. Over the deafening roar I could hear glass shattering as my dishes and lamps fell violently to the floor. I leaped out of bed and tried to make my way to a doorframe for protection, but the force of the shaking knocked me violently from wall to wall. I was desperately afraid, and my one thought was to reach the phone so I could call someone and not have to die alone. When I did reach the phone, it was dead.

The next major earthquake I endured occurred a few years later, when I was walking with the Lord. In marked contrast to the earlier quake, the instant this one hit the only One I thought to call was the Lord. Over the roar, I knew He heard my voice cry out for His help even when I could not hear it myself. I realized that He was there with me and, even if I died in that violent darkness, I would never be separated from Him.

Circumstances don't have to be catastrophic to be overwhelming. We can experience things that are nowhere near as life-threatening as what I just described, but can seem every bit as frightening. Some people view public speaking as a terrifying experience. They would rather endure an earthquake. For others, confronting a difficult person, having to make a dreaded phone call, or facing the daily challenge of an eating disorder or an addiction are earth-shaking challenges. Many people are overwhelmed by raising children, handling the responsibilities of life, or dealing with a strong-willed teenager.

Sometimes the pileup of many little things—each one alone being relatively harmless—becomes more than we can handle. Such things as stress in the workplace, pressure at school, uncomfortable social situations, or anything else that brings expectations that we feel we can't live up to can fill us with overwhelming anxiety. No matter what the specifics, the key to overcoming these kinds of overwhelming circumstances is to walk step by step with God through them.

When we set our anchor in the Lord, we will not be carried away by the storms that threaten to overtake us.

Godly people throughout the Bible, and anyone since who has not lost touch with reality, have all gone through times of being overwhelmed and fearful. Yet being afraid doesn't mean that God is not with you, that you are out of God's will, or that you are a spiritual weakling. It *could* be a sign that you are in the wrong place, doing the wrong thing, or that something is out of order in your life. It may also be an indication of enemy attack or a warning of a threat to your safety. If fear comes upon you without any apparent reason, ask God to show you what it means and where it is coming from. It may be a signal from the Lord to pray. That has happened to me many times, always for a good reason that I didn't understand until later.

One morning I woke up at three A.M. with tremendous fear. I asked God to show me what was causing it, then felt led to pray about the safety of my home and family. As I prayed for them, I sensed an urgency to also pray for the safety of the homes and families in our neighborhood. Then I covered the next neighborhood and the next, followed by our community, and finally the whole town. I had prayed many times before for all that. Just never at three in the morning. When the fear was gone, I went back to sleep.

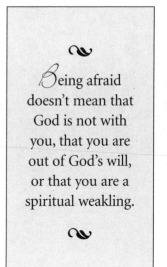

⌒

*B*eing afraid doesn't mean that God is not with you, that you are out of God's will, or that you are a spiritual weakling.

⌒

A few hours later, I was awakened by a phone call from a close friend telling us there were severe tornado warnings and that we should get into the basement immediately. We did. And the tornadoes came. They were all around us, but we were safe in the midst of them. Even in the area not far from us where the tornadoes did the greatest amount of damage, only one death occurred. I'm sure I wasn't the only one God woke up to pray, but when He did, I asked Him to show me what my fear meant and sensed Him leading me to intercede. Never underestimate the significance of praying through any unexpected and unexplained fear.

Don't ignore your fear, but refuse to be controlled by it. Sometimes the enemy of your soul will come upon you and in a moment show you *everything* you could possibly fear. When that barrage happens, don't listen to any of it. Tune out his lies and tune in to God's Word. Ask the Lord to speak to you, and He will tell you the truth.

Any sign of fear should always be a call to prayer. The moment you feel it, draw *immediately* close to God. Get a sense of His presence and leading and allow His love to fully penetrate your situation. Perfect love casts out all fear, but thank God it's not *our* love that has to be perfect. Only *His* can.

The deeper we press into the Lord, the more of His perfect love we experience, and the less fear we will have.

When your whole life is shaken, when the circumstances you face are so overwhelming that you feel like an ant in the face of Mount Everest, look to God and see *His* awesome power. Stand before the mountain and say, "Lord, where I am right now I declare

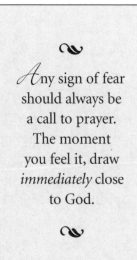

∾

*A*ny sign of fear should always be a call to prayer. The moment you feel it, draw *immediately* close to God.

∾

to be holy ground. I invite You to reign in this situation, for You are greater than anything I am facing. 'In Your light I see light'" (Psalm 36:9). Sense that His presence is with you to give you peace. There in the darkness of your earth-shaking circumstances, reach up to God and know that His mighty hand can reach forth to yours faster than the speed of light.

--- *Prayer Light* ---

*L*ord, I can only make it through this time if I walk closely with You. My days are in Your hands. While there are many things that can happen in life that are frightening or overwhelming, I know that Your power is greater than all of them. Even when what I experience is too much for me, it is never too much for You. Anything I face is nothing alongside Your ability to redeem it. Lord, I lift to You the things that frighten me most and ask that You would protect me and the people I love from them. Specifically, I bring before You, (name of overwhelming situation) and ask that You would work Your redemption in it. I know that my enemy is the one who "has made me dwell in darkness.... Therefore my spirit is overwhelmed within me. . . . Cause me to know the way in which I should walk, for I lift up my soul to You" (Psalm 143:3-4,8).

Whatever I need to do to make my path one of safety and peace, show me how and enable me to do it. Give me wisdom, strength, and clarity of mind to hear what You are saying to me in the midst of any dark or overwhelming situation. May my life be a testimony of the power of Your glory manifested as I walk in the light You have given me.

Footlights

Hear my cry, O God; Attend to my prayer.
From the end of the earth I will cry to You,
When my heart is overwhelmed;
Lead me to the rock that is higher than I.
For You have been a shelter for me,
A strong tower from the enemy.
I will abide in Your tabernacle forever;
I will trust in the shelter of Your wings.

PSALM 61:1-4

The LORD is my light and my salvation;
Whom shall I fear? The LORD is the strength
of my life; of whom shall I be afraid?

PSALM 27:1

In the day of my trouble I sought the Lord;
my hand was stretched out in the night
without ceasing; my soul refused
to be comforted. I remembered God,
and was troubled; I complained,
and my spirit was overwhelmed.
. . . Surely I will remember Your wonders of old.
I will also meditate on all Your work,
and talk of Your deeds.
. . . You are the God who does wonders. . . .

PSALM 77:2,3,11,12,14

There is no fear in love; but perfect
love casts out fear, because fear
involves torment. But he who fears has
not been made perfect in love.

1 JOHN 4:18

EIGHTEEN

Reaching for God's Hand in Times of Loss

Everyone experiences loss. It's a part of life. It's the part we don't like and wish we never had to go through. But we all will.

When our losses are severe, we feel like a light has gone out inside of us. And nothing can turn it back on except the restoration of that which is no more. It leaves a hole in our heart the size of the Grand Canyon. But even if what was lost can never be brought back, the part of our life that has died as a result *can* be made to live again. When we walk in the light of God's resurrecting power, He can soothe our pain, heal our wounds, and fill the empty places in our heart.

The worst time of loss for me was the day after my best friend's funeral. I had cried all the way through Diane's battle with breast cancer, her painful and agonizing death in the hospital, and her funeral where I tried to help her husband and eight-year-old son deal with their grief. But nothing compared to the devastation I experienced the morning after it was all over and the finality of it hit me.

It was Monday, the day Diane and I had always prayed together. It was unbearably hard to accept that we would never talk together again. Two days before that was my birthday, and it was the first time in the twenty-eight birthdays I'd had since we'd become friends in high school that I did not receive her early morning phone call telling me she was glad I was born. During some of those years, I believed she was the only one on earth who felt that way. I knew I'd never again have a friend on earth who knew me so well, and life would not be the same without her.

Before she died, I made her a promise that I would look after her son, John. So I kept busy taking care of him, along with my own two children, until his dad was able to pull their lives together and take him home to stay. When John left, I felt the loss all over again. I carried on with my life, but inside there was always a giant lump in my throat. After a couple of months, people didn't want to hear any more about it. I gathered there was an unspoken time limit for grief, after which everything had to return to normal. But I couldn't make myself follow the schedule. I stopped talking about it, not because the grief was any less, but because no one wanted to listen.

It wasn't until I finally gave up trying to deal with the grief myself and surrendered it to God that I began to find relief. As I walked step by step with Him through each day, He gave me the light I needed for that moment, that hour. He became my consolation. He led me to people who understood my loss, whose love and prayers brought healing. And my grief finally ended.

During the dark times of loss, whether it's the death of a loved one, a crippling disease or injury, divorce, a straying child, the end of a relationship, or the loss of home and finances, we grieve because someone or something we love is no longer part of us. Life as we once knew it is forever destroyed. The way we envisioned our future—with that person, with that security, with that capability—is severely shattered. These kinds of losses can bring such pain that we wonder if we will survive them, and, if we do, will we ever feel anything other than the pain? Will we hurt forever? Will life ever feel normal again?

While every act of compassion, sympathy, and love shown to us by others can be a great comfort and help to lift us out of our grief, only the healing touch of God can completely restore us again. We can't expect mere humans to say words that will make the pain go away. People don't always know the right words to say, and what words can make it better, anyway? It's the love in people's hearts, expressed however eloquently or awkwardly, that brings us comfort. If we get hung up on the words, we can miss the love behind them. When people are trying to show us love during our time of loss, we need to let them show it and not criticize them if they don't do it perfectly.

When we have suffered a deep loss, only God can sustain us, take the pain away, and make us whole again.

A tragic and needless death happened in my family over fifty years ago, but the wounds of those who deeply felt the loss are still as fresh today as they were then. The mere mention of that person's name immediately brings tears of grief, pain, and regret. That's because healing is still needed that only God can provide.

When we read the morning paper or watch the news on television, we hear of people suffering devastating loss and wonder how they will survive

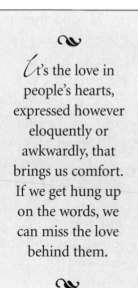

It's the love in people's hearts, expressed however eloquently or awkwardly, that brings us comfort. If we get hung up on the words, we can miss the love behind them.

it. How do the mothers and fathers who lose not one, but all of their children in a tragic accident live through it? My own cousin lost his wife and their three young children in a devastating flash flood. The pain he endured was beyond what should be the limit of human suffering. Nothing could ever take that pain away, nor heal the hole in the heart of this young man and his extended family. Several years after the tragedy he came to visit me, and I deeply regretted that I was not capable of offering any adequate words of consolation to him. I see now that nothing I could have said would have made any difference. Only the healing power of God's love could do that, and I didn't know enough about God then to help him as he needed to be helped.

Often people blame God for the tragedies in their lives and close themselves off from the very One who can take their pain away. But we won't make that same mistake if we will remember two things: God is good, and Satan comes to kill and destroy. It's crucial to not confuse the two during a time of loss.

If you suffer any kind of loss, don't try to get your arms around *it*. Let God get His arms around *you*. He knows your suffering and will give you the comfort of His presence and the healing balm of His love.

If you walk step by step with God through each day of your loss, in time this pain that seems to be without end will actually subside and you will know happiness again.

There is no medal given for getting over loss quickly, so don't try to rush the healing process. Submit to every stage of it. Waves of grief come and go and return again when you least expect them. Even when you begin to forget, something will suddenly remind you of what you lost and you will feel the pain all over again. Don't dread those times. Embrace the Lord *in* them. All moments traveled on this road will bring about another part of the healing. Every tear will cleanse a layer of the wound. Each memory will become a salve to the soul.

When a tragedy happens, it's normal to feel that life has come to a complete standstill. But actually it's life as you *knew* it that has stopped. Your new life, *without* that which was lost, is going forward. You just can't see it yet. Even though it's hard to imagine the future being any different than it is at that moment, healing and restoration are happening. You won't always feel this way. There *will* be an end. The loss may have been sudden, but the transition to your new life must be traveled one step at a time.

In times of loss, reach up and take your Heavenly Father's hand. He wants to comfort you and shoulder your grief. He wants to walk with you and bear your burdens. Seek His steadying arm moment by moment and He will draw you closer to Him. Even if your well of tears seems to never run dry, continue to walk in the light of God's presence and you *will* make it through the river of grief to the other side. If you can't see ahead, it's okay. God will not only provide enough light for your next step, He will also enable you to take it.

Prayer Light

Lord, only You can fill that empty place in the canyon of sorrow that has been left in my heart. You are the one constant in my life that can never be lost to me. All else is temporary and changing. I know You are a good God and Your love for me is endless. Help me to cast my whole burden of grief on You and let You carry it. Even though there are times when it feels like I can't live through the pain, I know You will sustain me. Enable me to get beyond it. I realize life must go on, and I ask You to help me take the next step I need to take today. Even though it's hard to imagine life without the pain I feel, with You all things are possible. Your healing power can restore anything—even a broken heart. Walk with me, Lord. I trust You to take my hand and lead me until I can feel Your light on my face and joy in my heart once again.

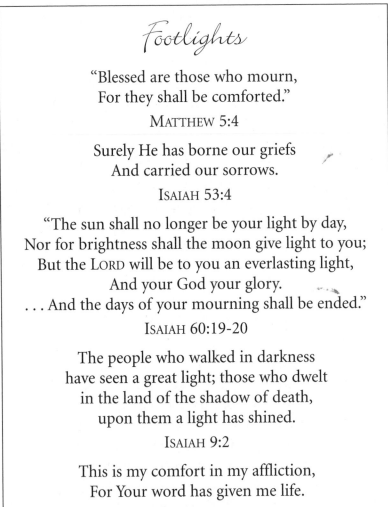

Footlights

"Blessed are those who mourn,
For they shall be comforted."

MATTHEW 5:4

Surely He has borne our griefs
And carried our sorrows.

ISAIAH 53:4

"The sun shall no longer be your light by day,
Nor for brightness shall the moon give light to you;
But the LORD will be to you an everlasting light,
And your God your glory.
. . . And the days of your mourning shall be ended."

ISAIAH 60:19-20

The people who walked in darkness
have seen a great light; those who dwelt
in the land of the shadow of death,
upon them a light has shined.

ISAIAH 9:2

This is my comfort in my affliction,
For Your word has given me life.

PSALM 119:50

NINETEEN

Stepping out of the Past

In order to live life successfully in the present and move into the future God has planned for us, we have to step out of the past. If we don't, it will color everything we see and affect all we do.

For example, if rejection has been part of your past and you haven't yet found God's healing for it, every experience you have will be interpreted through the eyes of rejection. It will be impossible to simply accept each moment for what it is without trying to read something else into it.

For the first thirty years of my life, I struggled with feeling that I would never be anything more than a failure. It was not until I entirely surrendered my past to the Lord, and walked out of it step by step, that I was able to see myself as a child of God created for *His* purposes and not a dysfunctional mistake. The biggest problem that faced me with regard to moving out of the past was unforgiveness.

Not forgiving the people and events of our past will keep us from ever being completely free of it.

Layers of unforgiveness began to be lifted as I forgave my mother for the abuse I suffered at her hands. She was mentally ill and coped with me by locking me in a closet during much of my early childhood. Even though she was verbally and physically abusive as well, the closet is what affected me the most.

When I became an adult, I was still locked in a closet emotionally. It wasn't until after I came to know the Lord and went to a Christian counselor for help with my depression that I was asked to acknowledge and confess the unforgiveness I had for my mother. When I did, I found freedom from the depression that had paralyzed me for years. As each layer of unforgiveness was stripped away, I became more and more liberated from the hurt and scars of the past.

In order to walk out of unforgiveness, we have to let go of everything except God's hand. This means releasing what needs to be released, and accepting what needs to be accepted. Even an incident that happened yesterday must be given to God so that it doesn't jeopardize our future. We can torture ourselves through the night with sleeplessness over something that happened only hours earlier. We can also live in so *distant* a past that we harbor unforgiveness today for people who hurt our ancestors generations ago.

We often refuse to let go of injustice and extend forgiveness to others simply because we can't receive the grace God extends to us through His forgiveness.

People who suffer from eating disorders, addictions, or any other destructive habits of the flesh that are rooted in the past often beat themselves up over reoccurring failure in their area of weakness. They can't forgive themselves and, as a result, the past controls their lives so much that they are unable to function successfully in the present. No matter what our past has been, it doesn't have to rule our lives today.

Beth had a serious problem with binge eating. As a result, her weight increased to a hundred pounds more than what was considered normal for her size. Even though the weight gain seriously compromised her health, she was unable to stop herself. She refused to get help because she had experienced failure in every weight loss program she had tried, and she believed that she would only fail again. It was a cycle from which she was never able to get free. Had she been able to fully receive God's love, grace, and forgiveness, her situation would have been different.

When we walk with the Lord, healing, deliverance, and growth are ongoing in our lives. That's why what may have been true for us last year will not necessarily be true for us today. Yesterday's failure may become today's success.

If there are things in your life about which you have a choice, yet you keep making the wrong choice over and over, you are probably living in the past in some way. There are no short-cuts to emotional healing, but it can happen if you get close to God and take one step at a time with Him. When you make Jesus Lord over your past and are willing to forgive yourself and everyone else associated with it, He can set you free. That means coming to Him every time you are tempted or tormented by the problem, and asking Him to help you move forward step by step.

We can get stuck in the negative complexities of the past when we

∞

We can get stuck in the negative complexities of the past when we don't recognize *our* part in it. We see injustices against us, but we fail to realize that at some point we are still responsible for our own attitudes.

∞

don't recognize *our* part in it. We see injustices against us, but we fail to realize that at some point we are still responsible for our own attitudes. If we live in fear, doubt, anger, hatred, resentment, bitterness, and unforgiveness over something that happened in the past—even if it does seem totally justified—we will suffer. We can't be in the dark about the issue of responsibility. Jesus came "to give light to those who sit in darkness and the shadow of death, to guide our feet into the way of peace" (Luke 1:79). We have to make peace with our past.

If you are in a place where you're not able to see a future for yourself, it may be because you believe the past has kept you from moving into the future God has for you. If you find yourself saying, "If only I had not done that"; "If only this had happened instead"; "If I had experienced that I would not be in this situation I am in today"; or "I have forever forfeited the kind of life that could have been mine," remember that these thoughts are not truth. The truth is that God redeems *everything*. Even our past. He meets us as we are swimming to keep our heads above the deep waters of past hurt and failure, and He brings us to the place we're supposed to be. He doesn't do it like a magic genie. He does it one step at a time as we depend on Him.

Getting free from our past doesn't happen overnight. It took me years to become completely free. After finally getting free of layer after layer of unforgiveness toward my mother, I found that I also harbored deep resentment toward my dad for never rescuing me from her insanity. That unforgiveness was so deeply buried in me that I was not even aware of it until I asked God to show me if it was there. Once I was set free of that, I came to a place of peace and productivity I had never before experienced.

Trying to come to terms with the past on your own can be difficult. That's why I advise people who have intensely hurtful pasts to seek the prayer and counsel of godly people who can help them find the healing and restoration God has for them. There is nothing wrong with asking for help. I went to counselors who knew God's truth, and had witnessed God's power, because they best understood how to pray for me. Don't hesitate to get godly counsel, but know that in the end it will be you and God together walking out of the past.

Once you step out of your past, don't look back. If you do, you may see a pattern of past failure that will color how you feel and affect the outcome of what you do today. It can make you fearful and faithless. "Let your eyes look straight ahead, and your eyelids look right before you. Ponder the path of your feet, and let all your ways be established. Do not turn to the right or the left; remove your foot from evil" (Proverbs 4:25-27).

Along with not looking back, it's not good to look too far ahead, either. Doing so may cause you to worry about where you think you *should* be, and that can be overwhelming too. Looking back, you see all that you *didn't* do. Looking too far forward, you see all you think you *can't* do. It's best to embrace the step you're on and say, "God, give me the ability to do what I have to do today."

As we resist being controlled by the negative part of our past, we should also not rely on the positives of our past. While it is right to remember the good things God has done in our lives, we are never to rest on last year's revelation and think we know it all. We need new revelation every day. Walking with God is an ongoing process. We reach plateaus along the way and God gives us a

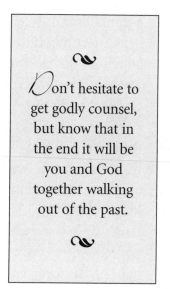

∾

*D*on't hesitate to get godly counsel, but know that in the end it will be you and God together walking out of the past.

∾

sabbath, but then He gets us up and moving on the path again. He never allows us to rest on our past success. If we did, we would become stagnant, prideful, or careless, and we would not be relying on Him.

The way we step out of the past is to walk in the Spirit. We are walking in the Spirit when the guide for our life is God's Word instead of magazines, television, movies, worldly books, or ungodly people. We are walking in the Spirit when we ask God daily for direction, guidance, and revelation. We are walking in the Spirit when we commit every aspect of our life—relationships, work, decisions, thoughts, and actions—to prayer instead of leaving it all to chance. We are walking in the Spirit when we determine each morning to worship God and set our mind on the things He has called us to, and not on things that have happened in the past.

If your past is an old familiar tune you've sung so long it's turned into the theme of your life, stop the music and ask God to put a new song in your heart. Check to see if you need to confess anything. While you may not have robbed a bank, committed murder, or had an affair, perhaps you have succumbed to doubt, criticism, self-pity, complaining, anger, or lovelessness. Until you are certain that you're washed clean by God's forgiveness, you are still swimming in the muddy waters of the past.

One of the descriptions of light is revelation. That's where the old familiar saying "Shine a light on the situation" comes from. When you need God to shine a light on your situation, ask Him for revelation. He will reveal anything you need to know, and give you understanding where you did not have it. Don't sit in the darkness of the past when God has laid out a path for you to walk in the present that is illuminated with the light of His forgiveness and revelation.

————————— *Prayer Light* —————————

*L*ord, I release my past to You. Everything I have done and all that was done to me I lay at Your feet. I give You my bad memories and ask that You would heal me to complete wholeness so that they no longer hurt, torment, or control me. Bring me to the point where my past, even as recent as yesterday, will in no way negatively affect today. I give You my past failures in the area of (<u>name any reoccurring problem</u>). Set me free from this. Even though I may be unable to completely resist the pull of certain things on my own, I know You are able to set me free. Make me a testimony to the power of Your healing and deliverance.

I confess any unforgiveness in my heart for things that have happened in the past, and I release all persons who are associated with it. I specifically forgive (<u>name of person I need to forgive</u>). Heal all misunderstandings or hurts that have happened between us and make things right. I know that I can never be free and healed if I tie myself to others by unforgiveness, so I ask You to bring to light any unforgiveness in me of which I'm not even aware. Give me Your revelation and show me all I need to see in order to walk out of the shadow of my past and into the light You have for me today.

Footlights

"Forget the former things; do not dwell on the past.
See, I am doing a new thing!
Now it springs up; do you not perceive it?
I am making a way in the desert
and streams in the wasteland."

ISAIAH 43:18-19 (NIV)

. . . the Lord will deliver me from every evil
work and preserve me for His heavenly kingdom.
To Him be glory forever and ever.

2 TIMOTHY 4:18

Therefore, if anyone is in Christ, he is a
new creation; old things have passed away;
behold, all things have become new.

2 CORINTHIANS 5:17

. . . You have delivered my soul from death.
Have You not kept my feet from falling,
that I may walk before God in the
light of the living?

PSALM 56:13

. . . put off, concerning your former conduct,
the old man which grows corrupt
according to the deceitful lusts, and be
renewed in the spirit of your mind,
and that you put on the new man which was
created according to God, in
true righteousness and holiness.

EPHESIANS 4:22-24

TWENTY

Maintaining a Passion for the Present

The phrase "timing is everything" is never more true than in your walk with God. However, it is most accurately stated, "*His* timing is everything."

When we come to a place where we trust that God's timing is perfect, we can be content no matter where we are because we know that God will not leave us there forever. Maintaining a passion for the present means embracing the light we have where we are at this time and trusting that it is enough.

I wrote some of this book during the early morning hours before dawn in various hotel rooms I have shared on the road with my husband or my daughter. So as not to disturb them, I used a tiny book light they gave me for my birthday. This light allows me to see only the line I'm on—the one I'm reading or the one I'm writing. In the past, I would have been very impatient with this arrangement because I didn't think I would have enough light to be able to work freely or quickly enough. But now, since I have learned to be content where I am with the light I am given,

...ence and am grateful for the light I do have. "For
...spised the day of small things?" (Zechariah 4:10).
... ...ght I have is enough for what I'm called to do right
now.

Being grateful for what we have doesn't mean we will
never have more. God doesn't say, "If you're so happy where
you are, I'll just leave you there." He continually keeps us
growing and moving along the path. If you are not in a
place you want to be right now, refuse to let that frustrate
or intimidate you. Pastor Jack Hayford says, "Don't let
where you are become a prophesy of where you're going to
stay."

I love that!

The *good* news is that if you are in an *uncomfortable*
place, God guarantees you won't stay there. It's just a matter
of time before things change. The *bad* news is that if you are
in a *good* place right now, it won't last forever. You'll soon
be moved into stretching beyond your comfort zone. Get
ready for the ride!

That's the way it is for a child of light who walks with
a leading from the Lord. "For you were once darkness, but now you
are light in the Lord. Walk as children of light" (Ephesians 5:8). Children of
light walk with God fully in control, and their steps are established because
they take them on solid ground.

People who walk with a leading from the Lord have a sense of purpose, which clearly marks the boundaries of their lives and makes their choices easy. They are more confident, more compassionate, more aware, and more in tune to what is

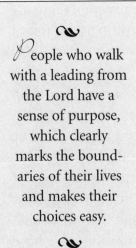

*P*eople who walk
with a leading from
the Lord have a
sense of purpose,
which clearly
marks the bound-
aries of their lives
and makes their
choices easy.

happening in the present. Too often we are so into our own lives that we don't see what is going on with someone who is right beside us. We become concerned with securing the future, and as a result we overlook the wealth of the present. But we don't want a "seat-of-our-pants" style of living where we barely make it through every aspect of our lives. We want to appreciate each stage of life and step we're on and live it fully. And that can only happen when we are led by the Spirit of God each day.

I believe the biggest midlife crisis happens when men or women lose the leading of the Lord. Or perhaps they never had it in the first place. So when they arrive at the point in their lives where they need it most, they run toward things they *think* will give them purpose, or at least disguise their lack of it, and they become lost.

When we don't have a clear leading from God, we can never be certain we are in His will. It's so much easier to be content with the step we're on if we know God has a purpose for us being there. People who are not certain about God's will for their marriage, for example, will give up and leave at the earliest indication of problems. They will never know the joy of going through the fire and getting to the glory. Too often we abandon the good in our lives for what appears to be greener pastures, all because we don't have the mind of Christ about it.

If God wants you in the place you are right now, then there are no greener pastures.

Walking with God means living moment by moment with Him in the present. Some people live in the past. Some people live for the future. Others give no thought to future or past, living only for the moment. We need to find a balance.

We must live in the present as if we don't have a past, certain that the steps we take today will determine our future.

Because our future is determined one day at a time in the present, we need to seek the leading of the Lord daily. We each have the ability to get off on our own little tangent. All it takes is a pound of presumption and a sprinkle of self-satisfaction glazed lightly with laziness, and we have the perfect recipe for missing the path.

One of the main purposes for our lives is to be extensions of God's light. He says, "Let your light so shine before men, that they may see your good works and glorify your Father in heaven" (Matthew 5:16). When we extend the light we have been given, it brings more light to our own lives. "If you extend your soul to the hungry and satisfy the afflicted soul, then your light shall dawn in the darkness, and your darkness shall be as the noonday" (Isaiah 58:10).

If I ever feel down and am tempted to wallow in the darkness of self-pity, I ask God to show me some way to extend His light to others. He always does. When I have shared such simple things as half a sandwich, an article of clothing, a ride, a phone call, a letter, a kind word, a touch, an apology, a prayer, a gift, a compliment, or a helping hand, I've seen the light on my path grow brighter each time.

Just as light from the moon is a reflection of the sun, the light we give off to others is a reflection of *God's* Son. As we look to Him, we reflect His light. When we allow God's light to shine through us, no matter how imperfectly we feel we do that, it not only shines on those around us but it illuminates our own path as well.

So let's do that! Let's free our lights to shine now—in this hour—no matter what we feel our wattage is. Let's live in the present believing what God says. If we need healing, let us

When we allow God's light to shine through us, no matter how imperfectly we feel we do that, it not only shines on those around us but it illuminates our own path as well.

turn to the Healer. If we need provision, let us turn to the Provider. If we need wisdom, let us ask the One who is all-wise. If we need love, let us receive God's love and pass it on to those around us. Let's not wait for *life* to be perfect before we live it. Let's not wait for *us* to be perfect before we start giving of ourselves. Let's not wait for *others* to be perfect before we start loving them. The time is now.

God says you are not to be anxious about tomorrow, for there will be plenty of things to concern you when you get there. You are to walk as a child of light, knowing that your future can only be reached one step at a time today. And you are to trust that He will give you the light you need, where you are right now, to take the right step.

Prayer Light

Lord, I want to live my life the way You want me to every day. Help me not to be stuck in my past, or so geared toward the future that I miss the richness of the present. Help me to experience the wealth in each moment. I don't desire to take a single step apart from Your presence. If You're not moving me, I'm staying here until I have a leading from You. I know I can only get to the future You have for me by walking one step at a time in Your will today. I realize there is no better time than the present to be Your light extended to those around me. Help me to get beyond myself and become an open vessel through which Your light can shine. Give me Your wisdom and revelation and show me all I need to see to keep me on the road You have for me. Enable me to step out of my past and keep an eye on the future by following Your light on my path today.

Footlights

The night is far spent, the day is at hand.
Therefore let us cast off the works of darkness,
and let us put on the armor of light.

ROMANS 13:12

. . . the LORD God is a sun and shield;
The LORD will give grace and glory;
No good thing will He withhold
From those who walk uprightly.

PSALM 84:11

". . . do not worry about tomorrow, for
tomorrow will worry about its own things.
Sufficient for the day is its own trouble."

MATTHEW 6:34

For I consider that the sufferings of this present
time are not worthy to be compared with the
glory which shall be revealed in us.

ROMANS 8:18

This is the day the LORD has made;
We will rejoice and be glad in it.

PSALM 118:24

TWENTY-ONE

Moving into Your Future

God has so much for us. We have no idea.

We look for crumbs under the table; He has prepared a feast for us in the royal banquet hall. We wonder if He remembers who we are; He has been calling our name. We wait for Him to notice our plight; He waits for us to take His hand. We see ourselves in the dark because we've done something wrong; He sees us in the light because we've done something right. He moves powerfully at our request; we don't even recognize the answers to our own prayers. We have trouble trusting Him fully with our future; the future He has for us is better than the one we dream of for ourselves. "Eye has not seen, nor ear heard, nor have entered into the heart of man the things which God has prepared for those who love Him" (1 Corinthians 2:9).

We worry so about our future because we can never be completely certain about it. A single event can change our lives. For the better, we hope. For the worse, we fear. But God says that, although we won't know everything about our future, we are still to inquire about it. "Ask Me of things to come . . ." (Isaiah 45:11), He instructs us. And when we ask, He sometimes reveals specifics. But most of the time He doesn't give us anything more than the assurance that our future is secure in His hands. He shows us that we *have* a future, and this simple knowledge must be enough for us.

The Bible says that Jerusalem's destruction came because "she did not consider her future" (Lamentations 1:9 NIV). The people did things with no thought of future consequences. We cannot do that. Living in the present doesn't mean we should not plan for what's ahead. We can and we must. We need to do whatever is necessary to plan and prepare for a child's education, next summer's vacation, a career, retirement, the weekend's activities, or our next meal. It's just that we are not to make plans without consulting God first and bringing Him into them. "A man's heart plans his way, but the Lord directs his steps" (Proverbs 16:9). W must never consider our future without first asking God to be in charge of it. And once we do that, we are to leave it in His hands and not lose sleep over it.

We must never consider our future without first asking God to be in charge of it. And once we do that, we are to leave it in His hands and not lose sleep over it.

I have a steep stairway in my house, and every time I look too far ahead when I walk up or down the steps, I stumble and fall. I don't have any problem when I pay attention to the step I'm on or the one that's just ahead. It's the same for our lives. Looking too far ahead can cause us to stumble. Some people look so far ahead into their future, it makes them afraid. It forces them to try to secure it on their own, and then they end up jeopardizing it by leaving God out of the picture. If God is not in our future plans, we spin our wheels in a scheme that doesn't have the potential to get off the ground, let alone fly.

I once knew a man who dashed frantically from one job to another, not because he needed the money, but because he was trying to make something happen for himself and secure his future. His commitment to the Lord was minimal; his obsession with success was paramount. His future is no more secure today than it has ever been, and he is still chasing after something that will forever elude him.

I know another man with the same kind of talent and abilities who chose to draw close to the Lord, humble and submit himself in every way, press into God's Word, and pray fervently for God's guidance. Doors flew open for him, some of which he didn't even dream of knocking on. He didn't try to make God fit *his* vision. He fit himself into *God's* vision. He didn't just do whatever he wanted to do, then ask God to bless it. He asked what *God* wanted him to do, and when he did it God blessed him.

Noah didn't one day decide he was going to build a giant boat and then, after he was finished, ask God to do something with it that would make him go down in history. Not at all. "Noah was a just man, perfect in his generations. Noah walked with God" (Genesis 6:9). This is worth repeating—*Noah walked with God.* And God bless him.

Abraham didn't suddenly say to Sarah one day, "Let's pull up stakes and wander in the desert, and then ask God to lead us somewhere." No, Abraham walked with God, and God told him to leave his country and go to a place He would show him. And God promised, *"I will bless you"* (Genesis 12:2). And God *did* bless him.

Moses didn't just decide one day to go to Pharaoh and ask him to release a million people so they could leave town together. No, Moses was quietly minding his own flock as

God had instructed him to do, when suddenly he heard the Lord call to him from the middle of a burning bush and *tell* him to go. When Moses waited for God's instructions, the Lord blessed everything he did.

These men were walking with God in their daily lives. God spoke to them and told them what to do. They did it. And God blessed them. Can there possibly be a lesson here for us?

You have a great future ahead and it will be reached as you move out of your past and walk step by step with God as He reveals Himself to you in the present.

Just as you should not live in the past, resist the urge to live in the future also. Put your future in God's hands, trusting that He will never withhold anything good from you, and then stop worrying about it. This doesn't mean a trumpet will sound announcing that you are spiritually immature if you find yourself concerned about the future. God is not asking you to be perfect. He is asking you to allow *Him* to be perfect in you. God is not asking you to have your whole future figured out. He is asking you to trust that *He* has your future planned. Thinking too much about the future can keep you from fully living the life God has given you now.

This doesn't mean you can't have goals. But some people have goals that are so strong they sacrifice everything to achieve them, even their family and God. Instead of allowing the goal to come *from* God, the goal itself *becomes* god.

Goals are not meant to be a plumb line to determine the shortest distance to success, but rather a compass to give a sense of direction.

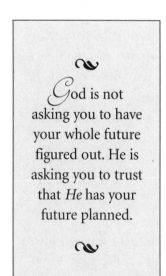

God is not asking you to have your whole future figured out. He is asking you to trust that He has your future planned.

If there is one goal I have for my future, it is that I will never again do what I regret having done in my past. And what I regret is every day I did not live for the Lord. I am sorry for anything I have done that has taken me away from His presence. I see it now as such a waste.

In hindsight, I realize that on every step of my life God has been there. Even when I didn't know Him. Even when I didn't realize I needed Him. Even when I was sure He couldn't possibly care. That's why I know He will be there for me in the future. And when I die, He will be there also. He will give me the light I need for that step, too. And I will weep, possibly for the times I didn't live for Him or believe what He said, but also because He didn't forget me. And He will dry my tears like He has promised to do, and I will live forever in the light of His presence.

The Lord will do the same for you. So keep your eyes on Him. Make Him your only source of light. Follow Him on that narrow pathway and you will be free. Free to trust Him for every step. Free to be all He made you to be. Free to do what He called you to do. Free to enjoy all He has for you. And you won't end up regretting the times you didn't live for Him, because there will no longer be any. You'll walk in a depth of love, peace, fulfillment, and joy you never thought possible.

You don't have to have your life all figured out; you only have to take one step at a time. God will give you just enough light for the step you're on, and every time you put your hand in His, you'll know you've got a solid hold on your future.

————————— *Prayer Light* —————————

Lord, I ask You to be in charge of my future. I don't want to dream dreams if You are not in them. I don't want to make plans that You will not bless. I don't want to work hard trying to harvest something that will never bear fruit because I did not receive the seed from You. Help me not to waste valuable time getting off the path and having to come back to the same place again. I don't want to get to the end of my life and regret the time I spent not living for You. Therefore I surrender my past, present, and future to You now.

Help me not be anxious about my future but to rest in the knowledge that my future is secure in You. I want to keep one foot in eternity by never letting go of Your hand. I want to store up so many treasures in heaven that heaven will feel familiar the moment I arrive. And when I do take that final step into my eternal future with You, I trust that You will be there for me with all the light I need for that step, too.

Footlights

. . . I know the thoughts that I think toward
you, says the LORD, thoughts of peace and not of evil,
to give you a future and a hope.

JEREMIAH 29:11

There is surely a future hope for you,
and your hope will not be cut off.

PROVERBS 23:18 (NIV)

Mark the blameless man, and observe the upright;
For the future of that man is peace.

PSALM 37:37

. . . I am persuaded that neither death nor life,
nor angels nor principalities nor powers,
nor things present nor things to come,
nor height nor depth, nor any other created
thing, shall be able to separate us from the
love of God which is in Christ Jesus our Lord.

ROMANS 8:38-39

"Arise, shine;
For your light has come!
And the glory of the LORD is risen upon you.
For behold, the darkness shall cover the earth,
And deep darkness the people;
But the LORD will arise over you,
And His glory will be seen upon you."

ISAIAH 60:1-2

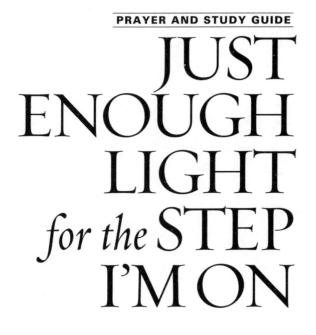

PRAYER AND STUDY GUIDE

JUST ENOUGH LIGHT
for the STEP
I'M ON

Welcome to the Journey

You are about to embark on a deeper walk with God. All you will need for the journey is a Bible that you feel free to write in. I have quoted from the New King James Version in the book, but you can use whatever translation you like.

What's the Answer?

The questions and directions in this prayer journey are designed to help you examine your walk with God and do whatever is necessary to strengthen and enhance it. Answer them as fully and completely as you can. Ask the Lord to help you as you write your answers, and you will be amazed how things you need to see will be revealed to you. Be sure to write something for each question or direction, even if it is only a sentence or two. And don't underestimate the power of writing out a prayer when asked to do so.

How to Proceed

This book is designed to be completed in the order it is laid out because one chapter builds upon another. While it is possible to skip around between different chapters, the impact will be greater if you follow the sequence as it is.

The Final Destination

The ultimate goal of this prayer journey is to help you see God in every circumstance and moment of your life, and to know with certainty that He is always there for you no matter what it feels like at the time. The purpose is also to encourage you to walk completely dependent upon the Lord for every step you take so He can get you where you need to go, which is far beyond where you can get on your own. And finally, my hope is that this study guide will help you know Jesus as the light of the world and be able to trust that, because you have received Him and surrendered your life into His hands, there is a light in you that can never be put out. This means you can live in confidence knowing you will always have the light you need for the step you're on.

WEEK *One*

Read Chapter 1: "Learning to Walk"

1. Describe how learning to walk with God is different from teaching a young child to walk. (See pages 11-12.)

2. Would you describe your walk with God as being very dependent, somewhat dependent, somewhat independent, or very independent? _____.
   Would you say your walk with God is close, distant, or somewhere in between? _____.
   How would you like to see your walk with God change? Name specific areas where you need to be more dependent on God. Write out a prayer asking God to help you walk closer to Him every day.

3. Read Joshua 3:11-17 and underline verse 13 in your Bible. According to this section of Scripture, the waters of the Jordan didn't part until what happened?

_____

_____.

(See also page 12, first paragraph.) God always requires the first step to be ours. Have you taken your first step with God by receiving Jesus into your heart? _____. Have you committed your life totally to Him? _____. If you haven't taken that first step, write out a prayer asking Jesus to come into your life and teach you how to walk with Him. If you have already received the Lord, write out a prayer telling God of your commitment to walk closely with Him and how you would like to see that commitment grow. Ask Him to show you any place in your life where you have not taken the steps He wants you to take.

4. Read Isaiah 30:18-21 and underline verse 21 in your Bible. When you are walking through difficult times, how will you know which way to go? _____

_____.

Have you ever been so afraid of taking the wrong step in your life that you did not take any steps at all? _____ If so, what was the end result of doing that? Write out a prayer asking God to help you hear His voice guiding you in the way you should go, and then enable you to take the necessary steps.

5. No matter how far away from God you've gone, when you surrender your life to _____, a _____ is carved from where you are to _____ and He puts you _____. (See page 13, second paragraph.) Can you think of a time when you have walked away from God? _____.

If you answered no, explain why. If you answered yes, what was the outcome of that? Have you ever felt that you have gotten so far off the path God had for you, either by your actions, thoughts, attitudes, or choices you've made, that you feel you could never arrive at the place God has for you? Describe.

6. As you take one _____ at a time, holding
   _____ hand and letting _____ lead, He
   will get you _____.
   (See page 14, first paragraph.) How willing are you to
   let God lead you where you need to go? _____.
   Do you ever doubt that God has your best interests at
   heart? _____.
   Is it ever tempting for you to take the reins of your life
   and not follow God's leading? _____. Explain
   your answers. Write out a prayer asking God to help
   you surrender your life totally into His hands so that
   He can lead you where you need to go.

7. Read Proverbs 16:9 and Psalm 37:23 and underline them in your Bible. According to these Scriptures, who directs our steps? _____. Why does God want you to become more and more dependent upon Him for every step? (See page 12, top of the page.)

_____

_____.

What are some of the things you would like to see happen in your life that you know can't happen unless God helps you to rise above certain obstacles?

8. God loves us so much that He allows us to get into
   _____ places in our lives so we will realize how
   _____ upon _____ we must be. (See
   page 16, first paragraph.) What is the most difficult
   situation in your life right now? Are you willing to
   depend on God to lead you through it or help you rise
   above it? Explain.

9. Read Hebrews 11:8 and underline it in your Bible. Have you ever experienced a time when you felt as though you had absolutely no idea where you were going in your life? _____. Do you feel that way now? _____. If so, does that make you feel concerned, or do you trust God so much that it doesn't bother you? Explain. Read Jeremiah 42:3 and underline it in your Bible. Describe your greatest concern about your future, and write out a prayer similar to the request for prayer in this section of Scripture, asking God to show you the way you should walk and the things you should do.

10. Pray the prayer out loud on pages 17-18. Include the specifics of your life that God has brought to your mind while studying this chapter.

WEEK *Two*

Read Chapter 2: "Beginning to See the Light"

1. Read 1 John 1:5-7 and underline these verses in your
   Bible. What is our true and unfailing source of light?
   _____.

   What are some of the things the light of the Lord does
   for our lives? (See page 21, last paragraph.)

2. Read 2 Corinthians 11:14 and underline it in your
   Bible. According to this verse, what other source of
   light competes for our attention? _____.
   Can you think of a specific time in your life when you
   have been misled by the light of the enemy and have
   not stayed in the light of the Lord? Explain. Write out
   a prayer confessing that as sin, and ask God to give
   you the ability to discern the deceptive tactics of the
   enemy.

3. Unless we follow the true light, we are being led into
   _____. (See page 22, first paragraph.) God's
   light is constant because _____.
   (See page 23, first paragraph.) God does not have us
   follow a light, He has us follow _____. (See
   page 23, top of page.) Can you think of an example
   from your own life when you went through a dark or
   difficult time and you began to doubt that God was
   there for you? Explain. Write out a prayer asking God
   to help you never doubt Him again.

4. Read John 8:12 and underline it in your Bible. Say the words of Jesus out loud three times. Whenever you enter into a dark time in your life, it is easy to forget that you have the light of the world in you that never goes out. At these times it will help if you are able to quote this verse. Write out the words of Jesus in John 8:12 three times below.

5. Can you think of a situation in your life right now where you especially need God to shine His light on your path as you walk through it? Explain. Write out a prayer asking God to help you trust His ability to fully illuminate this situation.

6. Read John 12:46 and underline it in your Bible. According to this verse, why is there no longer any reason for you to live in darkness?

7. Can you think of a time when it seemed to you as though God's light had grown dim in your life? What do you think was the reason for it? (For example, spending too much time around unbelievers, erratic church attendance, not reading the Bible, etc.)

8. Can you think of anything outside of the Lord that you have looked to as a source of light, especially during difficult times in your life? Explain.

9. What are some of the ways you can connect with the Lord? (See page 24, last paragraph.) In what ways do you feel you need to connect with God in a deeper way? (For example, to be more in the Word, to spend more time in prayer, etc.)

10. Pray the prayer out loud on page 26. Include the specifics of your life that God has brought to mind while studying this chapter.

Week *Three*

Read Chapter 3: "Refusing to Be Afraid of the Dark"

1. What are some of the different kinds of darkness? (See page 29, second paragraph.) Can you think of any ways in which you might be living in darkness in your life? _____. If you answered yes, what are they? If you answered no, write out a prayer asking God to show you if there is any way in which you have allowed darkness to penetrate your life. Write down what He reveals to you.

2. Read Psalm 107:10-11 and underline these verses in your Bible. According to this section of Scripture, why were the people sitting bound up in the dark?

3. Read Psalm 107:13-14 and underline these verses in your Bible. How were the people freed of their bondage and brought out of the darkness? _____ _____.

Is there any place in your life where you need to cry out to God and ask Him to deliver you? Explain. Write out a prayer asking God to set you free from this problem. Be specific.

4. Describe how you regard the presence of God in your life. Do you have such complete certainty about God's presence that even when you can't feel it, sense it, or see it, you know He is there? Explain. Write out a prayer asking God to give you a greater sense of His presence than you have ever had before.

5. One of the ways God makes us certain of His light is by allowing us to test it in the _____. (See page 30, last paragraph.) Can you think of a time in your life when you went through a difficult situation and God used it to draw you closer to Him and mature you in His ways? Explain. What did that do for your faith in God?

6. Read Isaiah 45:3 and underline it in your Bible. Why does God give us the treasures of darkness? _____
   _____.
   What is the treasure we find in darkness? _____
   _____. (See page 31, fourth paragraph.)

7. Compare what it's like when the power goes out in your home at night with how God uses darkness in your life. (See page 31, first and second paragraphs.) Is there a difficult situation you are going through right now where you need to reach out to God and ask Him to turn the situation around? Explain.

8. Sometimes what seems like the darkest step we've ever been on comes just before _____
_____.
(See page 33, second paragraph.) Can you think of an example in your life where a situation seemed to be at its lowest point just before it turned around and got better? How did that affect your faith at the time? Explain.

9. The unknown can be frightening, but when we immerse ourselves in the presence of the Lord, we can know _____ in it. His love takes away our _____. (See page 35, first paragraph.) Name specific areas of your life where fear has tormented you or kept you from walking victoriously. Then write a prayer asking God to set you free from that fear.

10. Pray the prayer out loud on page 36. Include the specifics of your life that God has brought to mind while studying this chapter.

WEEK *Four*

Read Chapter 4: "Embracing the Moment"

1. Read Philippians 4:11 and underline it in your Bible. Are there any areas in your life where you feel discontent? Explain. Write a prayer asking God to help you be content where you are and to trust that He won't leave you there forever.

2. Regardless of what your situation is at this moment,
   God has _____.
   (See page 41, second paragraph.) Is there any situation in your life right now where you need God to
   help you see His hand of blessing in it? Explain. Write
   out a prayer asking God to reveal His goodness in the
   situation.

3. God wants you to trust Him so much that when you are afraid, you can turn to Him and find _____. When you are weary, you can find _____. When you are empty, you can find _____. When you are sad, you can find _____. When you are in the middle of a storm, you can find _____. (See page 41, second paragraph.) Is it your first instinct to look for the goodness of God in the midst of your circumstances? Explain why or why not.

4. Why does God not want to give us too much light all at once? (See page 41, fourth paragraph.) Write a prayer asking God to help you be grateful for the light He gives you in each situation.

5. When you go through difficult experiences, are you filled with fear and doubt or do you have a strong sense of God's sustaining presence? Explain. Write out a prayer asking God to give you more faith to trust Him and sense His presence during the tough times in your life.

6. Have you ever felt great loneliness or are you feeling loneliness now? If so, to what degree is it a point of pain in your life? Are you able to see the loneliness that you feel as a call from God beckoning you to spend more time with Him? Is there any other negative emotion you are feeling because you are not trusting God? Explain.

7. Read Psalm 139:1-18 and underline every verse that speaks comfort to you. From this section of Scripture, do you think God knows you and where you are at any given moment? _____. Do you think He cares about you and your circumstances? _____. What do these verses speak to you about the situations you are facing in your life right now?

8. Read 2 Corinthians 4:17-18 and underline these verses in your Bible. What things are temporary? ___

_____.

What things are eternal? _____

_____.

Can you think of a difficult time in your life where good came out of it? Describe. What did that do for your faith in God?

9. Write down the most difficult thing you are facing at this moment in your life. Then list all of the good things you see in the midst of it. Write a prayer asking God to show you any good that you are *not* seeing, and then write down what He shows you.

10. Pray the prayer out loud on page 44. Include specifics of your life that God has brought to mind while studying this chapter.

WEEK *Five*

Read Chapter 5: "Dancing in the Footlights"

1. Read Psalm 119:105 and underline it in your Bible. According to this verse, what lights the path where we should be walking? _____. Unless the light of _____ is shining on your steps, you are walking in _____. (See page 47, third paragraph.) When we read _____, it lights our _____ and keeps us _____. Walking step by step with _____ can only be done successfully if we have _____ showing us the way. (See page 49, top of the page.)

2. How often do you read the Bible? _____ Do
   you feel it is enough? _____ How would you
   like to see your practice of being in God's Word
   change? Write out a prayer asking God to help you
   grow in the knowledge of His Word.

3. Read Psalms 119:130 and 119:165 and underline them
   in your Bible. According to these Scriptures, what
   does God's Word give you? _____ When
   you read God's Word, do you have more peace, clarity, security, or direction? _____. If you
   answered no, write out a prayer asking God to make
   His Word come alive in you and speak to your heart
   whenever you read it. If you answered yes, write out a
   prayer asking God to help you understand and retain
   His Word in greater depth than you have ever known
   before.

4. Read Matthew 4:1-11 and underline verses 4, 7, and 10 in your Bible. As Satan tempted Jesus in the wilderness, what did Jesus use as a weapon to refute everything the devil said? _____.
   Do you ever sense you are facing a spiritual battle where you need a powerful weapon to combat the enemy's lies and plans? Explain in detail. Write out a prayer asking God to help you learn to use His Word as a weapon to destroy the works and lies of the enemy.

5. Have you ever experienced times of fear, anxiety, depression, or unrest in your soul? Do you ever feel as if you are in the dark about where you are going in your life? Describe. What happens to you when you read the Word of God and speak it out loud in the face of that? Are you able to find relief, deliverance, or direction for your life? If you have not done that, do it now and then describe what happened as a result.

6. God's love letter, which is His Word, is a _____, a _____, and a _____. (See the subheads on pages 48, 50, and 51.) Which of those three things do you most need the Word of God to be to you today? Explain why.

7. The key to receiving the full message in God's love letter is to _____. (See page 48, second to the last paragraph.) Explain what happens when people read the Bible but have no relationship with and no love for God. (See page 48, top half of page.) Then write a letter to God telling Him how much you love Him and how much His love letter means to you.

8. Read Psalm 43 and underline verses 3 and 4 in your Bible. Do you ever feel you need to be free from any unjust, deceitful, or ungodly people? _____ Do you ever sense oppression from the enemy of your soul? _____ Do you ever feel downcast or anxious? _____ According to verses 3 and 4, what is the answer to these needs?

9. Read Hebrews 4:12 and Romans 15:4 and underline them in your Bible. In light of these verses, what can the Word of God accomplish in your life?

10. Pray the prayer out loud on page 52. Include the specifics of your life that God has brought to mind while studying this chapter.

WEEK *Six*

Read Chapter 6: "Paying Your Light Bill"

1. When we obey God we are _____, we
   hear _____, we see _____,
   and we can be _____. (See subheads on
   pages 58, 59, and 60.) When we *don't* obey God, one
   of the consequences is _____. (See
   page 55, second paragraph from the bottom.) Often
   we find ourselves walking in the dark simply because
   _____.
   (See page 55, last paragraph.) The price God requires
   for enjoying the fullness of His light is _____.
   (See page 56, first paragraph.)

2. Read Ephesians 2:8-10 and underline these verses in your Bible. What does receiving God's salvation cost us? _____. By what have we been saved? _____. Who paid the price for us? _____. But the price we have to pay for enjoying the fullness of His light and all He has for us is that we have to

_____.

(See page 56, second paragraph.)

3. We usually know if we are rebelling against God's laws. Are you aware of any of God's laws that you are not obeying? _____. If you answered yes, write out a prayer asking God to help you specifically walk in obedience in all areas of your life. If you answered no, write out a prayer asking God to show any place in your life where you are not walking in complete obedience to His ways.

4. Sometimes our disobedience can be so subtle that we are not even aware of it. Some of the things that can act like a riptide to carry us off course in our lives are: the cares of _____the influence of _____, _____, _____, _____, ignorance of _____, or our _____. (See page 57, third paragraph.) What are some of the subtle things in *your* life that compete for your attention and try to get you off course? Explain. Write out a prayer asking God to show you if you are not sure. Then write down what He reveals to you.

5. Read John 3:20-21 and underline these verses in your Bible. According to this section of Scripture, what happens if we practice disobedience? _____

_____.

What happens when we are doing what God says to do in His Word? _____

_____.

Do you feel that you are living in the light or in the dark or somewhere in between? _____

Are there any dark spots of disobedience you would like to see exposed to the light? _____

Explain. If you are not sure, write out a prayer asking God to show you if there is any area of disobedience you are walking in. (Remember that disobedience can happen if God is speaking to your heart about something you are to do and you are not doing it.)

6. Read Genesis 7:1 and underline it in your Bible. Why did God call Noah into the ark? _____
_____.
Noah's _____ ultimately saved him and his family from destruction. When we love God enough to obey what He asks, we come under
_____.
(See page 58, second paragraph.) Have you ever found yourself in the wrong place at the wrong time because you didn't do what God was telling you to do? Explain. Have you ever made a decision without asking Him to show you what to do? What was the outcome?

7. Read Proverbs 3:32 and underline it in your Bible. According to this verse, to whom does God give counsel? _____. Do you need the counsel of God about anything? _____ Do you need God's direction for any area of your life? _____. Write out a prayer asking God for direction and revelation. Be specific.

8. God reveals _____ to us in greater dimensions when we are _____

_____.

(See page 59, second paragraph.) Is there anything God is speaking to you specifically about which would require a particular step of obedience? Explain. If you are not sure, write a prayer asking God to reveal it to you.

9. Read 1 John 3:22 and underline it in your Bible. In light of this verse, is there a correlation between obedience and unanswered prayer? _____

Write out a prayer asking God to show you any area of disobedience in your life that is keeping your prayers from being answered. Write down what He reveals to you, if anything.

10. Pray the prayer out loud on pages 61-62. Include the specifics of your life that God has brought to mind while studying this chapter.

WEEK *Seven*

Read Chapter 7: "Standing in the Line of Fire"

1. Read Ephesians 6:10-13 and underline these verses in your Bible. According to this section of Scripture, who is it we do not wrestle against? Who do we wrestle against? How do we stand against them?

2. Do you recognize any instance in your life where you have wrestled against people instead of focusing on the enemy? Explain. Write out a prayer asking God to show you if there is a situation like that in your life right now and how you should pray about it. Write down what God reveals to you.

3. When you are under spiritual attack from the enemy, what is the thing that will keep you from panic? ____
_____.
(See page 65, second paragraph.) When we consistently live close to _____, we have the peace and confidence of knowing who is our _____ and who is our _____. (See page 65, third paragraph.) When God goes to battle for you, He doesn't stop until _____
_____.
(See page 66, second paragraph from the bottom.) Because any opposition we face from the enemy has spiritual power behind it, the battle must first be fought in _____ before victory will be seen in _____. That means we need to _____. (See page 67, top of the page.)

4. Read 2 Chronicles 20:15 and underline it in your Bible. When you are facing opposition, whose battle is it? _____. Is there any place in your life right now where you feel the enemy is opposing you or one of your immediate family members? _____ Write out a prayer declaring your dependence upon God in this situation. Thank Him for His goodness and power toward you and ask Him to fight the battle for you as you give Him the glory.

5. Read Exodus 14:13-14 and underline these verses in your Bible. Who will fight for you when you are battling the enemy? _____. Can you think of a time when you prayed for God to help in a difficult situation and you knew that God fought the battle for you? Explain. If you have never had that experience, write out a prayer asking God to fight whatever battle you are facing now or will face in the future.

6. Read Psalm 17:7-9 and underline these verses in your Bible. What did David ask God to do for him? _____.

   Is there any area of your life where you feel there may possibly be a battle ahead and you need God to fight it for you? _____ Explain. Then write a prayer asking God to fight this battle for you while He hides you in the shadow of His wing.

7. At the first sign of enemy attack, go to _____ and listen to what _____. (See page 68, second paragraph from the bottom.) The moment you realize you are standing in the line of fire, recognize who _____, and run to _____. Let the song of _____ and _____ rise in your heart as you watch the _____ defeat the _____ on _____. (See page 70, first paragraph.)

8. Is there any place in your life right now where the enemy is attacking you? If so, write out words of praise to God regarding that situation. Thank Him that He will deliver you from the hands of the enemy.

9. Have you ever felt alone in the battles you face? _____. When you walk with the Lord in the battle, can you ever really be alone? _____. Why? _____. Why does God sometimes wait until the eleventh hour to rescue us in the heat of battle? What are we to do when that happens? (See page 69, last two paragraphs.)

10. Pray the prayer out loud on pages 70-71. Include specifics of your life that God has brought to mind while studying this chapter.

WEEK Eight

Read Chapter 8: "Seeing What's Right with This Picture"

1. Read Romans 8:28 and underline it in your Bible. Do you really believe this verse? _____
   Explain why or why not in light of your experience. Do you believe you are called according to God's purpose for you? _____. Do you love God? _____. Write out a prayer telling God how much you love Him, and thank Him that He will bring good out of every situation in your life. List the situations in your life that you are especially concerned about.

2. Seeing what's right with this picture means searching for _____ and seeing reality from _____. (See page 74, second paragraph from the bottom.) Can you think of a situation that is having a negative effect on your life right now? Write out a short prayer asking God to show you the situation from *His* perspective.

3. Describe the most difficult situation in your life at this moment. Then list all the things that are good and right about the situation. Find the positive side of any negative aspect. If you can't find any, ask God to show you and write down what He reveals.

4. Often we pray for something and don't even recognize the _____

_____

because it does not _____

_____.

(See page 77, second paragraph.) Can you think of a situation in your life where you failed to recognize an answer to your prayers? If so, describe it. If not, write a prayer asking God to show you if you have ever failed to recognize an answer to your own prayer because it wasn't answered the way you thought it would be.

5. Read Psalm 34:8 and underline it in your Bible. Do you have complete trust that God is a good God and you can trust Him completely with your life? Explain your answer.

6. Read Psalm 27:13-14 and underline these verses in your Bible. Are there places in your life where you have lost hope that things will ever turn out the way you want them to? Explain. What does God's Word say to do?

7. Read Psalm 115:5 and underline it in your Bible. This verse is talking about the idols in our lives. They can't see our situations, and they can't speak life into us. But God can. So why would we want to look to anything outside the Lord to help us? Have you ever become so discouraged because of unanswered prayer that you took matters into your own hands and looked to a source other than God to make it happen? Explain. What was the outcome of that? Did that indicate an idol in your life? Write out a prayer telling God about any prayer you have prayed that you feel has gone unanswered. Ask Him to show you if the answer has already come and you didn't see it.

8. Read Psalm 116:1-2 and Psalm 118:24 and underline them in your Bible. Write these three verses out as a prayer to God. (For example, "Lord, I love You because You have heard my voice…" etc.)

9. Read Psalm 112:1-8 and underline in your Bible the verses that especially speak to you, then explain in your own words why you don't have to be afraid of bad news or difficult times that may come in the future.

10. Read the prayer out loud on page 78. Include the specifics of your life that God has brought to mind while studying this chapter.

Week *Nine*

❧

Read Chapter 9: "Testing, One, Two, Three"

1. What are the three major tests God puts us through?
_____, _____, and
_____. (See the subheads on pages
84, 85, and 86.) Do you feel you have ever been tested
in any one of these areas? Explain.

2. What is the purpose of God's tests? How are they different from the tests we took in school? (See page 81.)

3. When are we often put to the most difficult tests?

_____.

(See page 82, second paragraph.) Can you think of a time in your life when you were put through a difficult test and soon afterward there was great breakthrough and blessing in your life? During that testing process, did you ever come close to giving up? Explain.

4. Read Matthew 5:8 and underline it in your Bible. Can you think of a situation that you have gone through that served to purify your heart and helped you to see and know God better? Are you possibly going through such a time right now? Explain. What do you think will make the difference between becoming purified or becoming bitter when you are going through a difficult trial?

5. Read James 1:2-4 and underline these verses in your Bible. What is the ultimate result of having your faith tested? Do you find it easy or hard to have joy in the midst of the trials you go through? Have you been perfected in being patient? Explain.

6. Read Exodus 20:20 and underline it in your Bible. What is another reason God tests us? Do you believe that in the trials and tests you have gone through you have developed a healthy fear of the Lord, which has kept you from sin? Explain.

7. Can you think of an area of your life where you have been tested on your obedience? Explain. Has God ever convicted your heart about something and you were reluctant to do what He asked you to do? Explain. What was the outcome?

8. Read Psalm 66:8-12 and underline these verses in your Bible. What is accomplished in our lives when we are tested?

9. According to Psalm 66:8, what should be our reaction to the times of testing God puts us through? Is your first reaction to difficult times an attitude of praise and worship? Explain why or why not. Write out a prayer asking God to help you make praise to Him your first reaction to any situation.

10. Pray the prayer out loud on page 88. Include the specifics of your life that God has brought to mind while studying this chapter.

WEEK Ten

Read Chapter 10: "Knowing How
to Pack for the Wilderness"

1. The wilderness is where we are forced to leave behind
   the _____, the _____,
   the _____, the _____,
   and the _____. God wants to separate
   us from _____ so that all we crave is
   _____. God doesn't want us to depend on
   what's comfortable, He wants us to depend on
   _____. When God aims us in a new direction,
   we have to let go of _____, be willing
   to _____, and trust that He will
   _____. (See page 93, first para-
   graph.)

2. Read John 10:27 and underline it in your Bible. Do you feel you are one of God's sheep who hears His voice? _____. Are you willing to follow Him wherever He leads? _____. Write a declaration of your commitment to follow the Lord, even if it means you will have to leave the familiar and the comfortable.

3. Read Mark 8:34 and underline it in your Bible. Have you ever had to leave a job, a house, friends, a church, family members, or anything else that you loved in order to follow the leading of the Lord? Describe the experience. What was the outcome? Did it make you more or less dependent upon God?

4. In the wilderness, the Israelites had to gather manna each day to sustain them. What is the manna *we* have to take in each day to sustain us?_____

_____.

(See page 95, first paragraph.) Do you seek the Lord's presence each day by spending time in His Word, praise, and prayer? Does your time spent with Him feed your soul and help you to be content with the moment? Explain why or why not.

5. Read Exodus 33:15 and underline it in your Bible. This verse quotes what Moses said to God regarding his leading the Israelites from Egypt to the Promised Land. Do you feel that you, too, would not want to make a move in any direction unless you knew that the presence of God was going with you? Write out a prayer in your own words expressing that thought to God.

6. The wilderness is a place where God calls us to
_____ and move into
the _____ so He can guide us
_____. (See page 95, top of the
page.) Has God ever asked you to give up some of
your comforts and take a step of faith as you move
out into the unknown? What was your response? Is
He asking that of you now? Explain. How do you feel
about it?

7. Do you feel you are in a wilderness situation now in your life, or have you been so in the past? Describe that experience. Have you been able to see the goodness of the Lord during that time? Explain. The purpose of the wilderness is not for God to punish you, but it is so God can purify you, make your roots go down deep in Him, and prepare you for what He has for you. Do you feel your wilderness time has done that, or is doing that, for you? Explain.

8. Why does God seldom reveal our final destination when He takes us to a new place in our lives? (See page 94, first and second paragraphs.) How could the Israelites' wilderness experience have been a shorter one? (See page 94, last paragraph.)

9. Write out a prayer asking God to help you know Him in a deeper sense than ever before. Tell Him you want His presence more than anything else on earth.

10. Pray the prayer out loud on page 97. Include the specifics of your life that God has brought to mind while studying this chapter.

WEEK *Eleven*

Read Chapter 11: "Surrendering Your Dreams"

1. What is your greatest dream or the deepest desire of your heart today? Describe in detail.

2. Have you surrendered your dream to the Lord?
   _____. If you haven't, would you be willing to
   now? _____. Whether you have already surrendered it or not, write a prayer releasing your dream
   into the Lord's hands. Tell Him you are willing to die
   to it completely and allow Him to take away any
   desire for it if that is not His will for you. Ask Him to
   resurrect it and make it happen if it *is* in His will to do
   so.

3. Read John 15:1-5 and underline these verses in your Bible. How much can you accomplish without the Lord? _____ Have you ever had a dream that you had to let die? _____. What was it? Do you think you had to let go of that dream because you were being pruned, or was it something you weren't supposed to have? In light of this section of Scripture, could it be because God wanted you, the branch, to learn to abide in Him, the true Vine, before you could bear fruit? (See verse 5.) Explain.

4. Do you have gifts and talents that you feel have not been developed or used as they should be? Explain. Describe how you would feel about that. What would you like to see happen with regard to these gifts and talents.

5. Read Psalm 37:4 and underline it in your Bible. What must you do for God to give you the desires of your heart? _____

_____.

Why should we surrender all of our dreams and desires to Him first? (See page 100, first paragraph.)

6. Read 1 Corinthians 13:2-3 and underline these two
   verses in your Bible. According to them, how much
   can you accomplish in your life if you don't do it in
   love? _____.
   Describe your attitude with regards to surrendering
   the dreams and desires of your heart to the Lord. Has
   it been easy? Or have some dreams died hard? Then
   write a prayer asking God to help you do that with
   total joy and peace. Ask Him to help you have the
   patience and faith to wait on Him to reveal His will
   for your life.

7. We don't want to be just wishful thinkers. We want to live with confidence that our hopes, dreams, and expectations are based on _____ _____.
We want the hope that comes _____
and is built on a foundation of _____.
This kind of hope is an _____
_____.
(See page 102, first paragraph.) If you agree with the statements above, write a prayer asking God to help you have that kind of certainty about your hopes and dreams.

8. Read Romans 8:25 and underline it in your Bible. What do you hope for that you do not see? Do you ever lose hope and stop praying about it? Explain. Write a prayer asking God to help you persevere according to His will and not lose hope. (When you know your hopes are in alignment with God's will, you are strengthened to persevere in prayer about them.)

9. Read Psalm 28:6-7 and underline these verses in your Bible. Even though you may have prayers that have gone unanswered, do you believe that you can trust that God always hears them? God's Word gives you confidence to know that as long as you are praying, the situation is in God's hands. Write out a prayer thanking God for hearing your prayers and praise Him for the answers, whatever they may be. God wants to know that you care more about what *He* wants than what you want. Tell Him you do.

10. Pray the prayer out loud on pages 104-105. Include the specifics of your life that God has brought to mind while studying this chapter.

WEEK *Twelve*

Read Chapter 12: "Waiting in the Wings"

1. Is there any area of your life where you have been waiting for something to happen? Have there been times in the past when you waited a long time for something important to take place? Describe the experience and how you responded to the waiting period. What was the outcome? How do you feel about it?

2. Read Lamentations 3:25-26 and underline these two
   verses in your Bible. What do they say about those
   who wait? _____.
   It's best to view waiting times by thinking of them as
   times of _____. (See page 108, first
   paragraph.) Regarding the area of your life where you
   are waiting for something to happen, write a prayer
   releasing it into the Lord's hands and telling Him you
   will wait on *Him* instead of waiting for things to
   change.

3. Read Isaiah 40:31 and underline it in your Bible. Write this verse as a prayer about your life. (For example, "Lord, help me to wait on You so that I can renew my strength…" etc.)

4. Does going through a waiting period mean there is nothing happening in your life? Explain. What direction are you always going in when you are walking with the Lord? (See page 109, second and third paragraphs.)

5. Make a list below of some of the things you can be doing while you are waiting on the Lord. (For example, studying and meditating more in God's Word, helping others, etc.) Be specific.

6. According to Psalm 27:14, what happens when you wait on the Lord instead of just waiting for things to happen?

7. Why is it important to keep praying while you are waiting on the Lord, even though you may be praying about the same thing over and over? (See page 110, first paragraph.) Explain.

8. Read Psalm 37:3-8 and underline these verses in your Bible. What should you be doing as you wait on the Lord? (For example, "I should be trusting in the Lord and doing good…" etc.)

9. Do you think there is any area in your life where you are waiting for something to happen, but God is possibly waiting on *you* to take action first? Explain what you see to be true about yourself with regard to this. If you are not sure, write out a prayer asking God to show you where you need to be taking certain steps. Then write down what He shows you.

10. Pray the prayer out loud on page 111. Include the specifics of your life that God has brought to mind while studying this chapter.

WEEK *Thirteen*

Read Chapter 13: "Expecting a Call"

1. Do you have a sense that you were created for a great purpose or calling? If so, what is that purpose or calling as far as you understand it?

2. With regard to your purpose and calling, do you feel hopeful anticipation of what is to unfold in your life, or do you feel hopeless regret that God might never be able to do something significant through you? Or does what you feel about this fall somewhere in between those two extremes? Explain your answer.

3. Read 1 Peter 2:9 and underline it in your Bible. For what purpose have you been chosen and called out of darkness? _____

_____.

Do you feel you are fulfilling that purpose or calling? Explain.

4. Read Romans 11:29 and underline it in your Bible. Do you think it will ever be too late for you to use the gifts God has given you to move into the calling He has for you? _____. Why? Read also verse 36 of Romans 11 and explain what that verse speaks to you with regard to your calling.

5. Are you able to see how your calling can be worked out in the details of your life the way it is now? _____. If you answered yes, write a prayer asking God to enable you to fulfill the calling He has on your life. If you answered no, write a prayer asking God to take your life as it is and use it powerfully for His purpose.

6. Did you ever sense that you were called to something greater than what you were doing at the time, but nothing materialized in that regard? _____. How did you respond to that? Did you remain hopeful or become hopeless. What are some of the reasons God might take you through a waiting period? (See page 117.)

7. What are some of the ways *we* think reveal greatness, but are not what *God* believes to be signs of greatness? (See page 118, first paragraph.) List those ways and indicate which ones, if any, you have been influenced to think were signs of greatness.

8. God's idea of greatness is having a _____,
_____, and _____ so full of
_____ that it manifests through
_____. (See page 118, second paragraph.)
Greatness is not about us, it's about _____
_____. (See page 118, first paragraph.)
In light of your answers, what are the conditions you
need to have in your life in order for God to do something great through you? Are those conditions something you have some control over? Explain.

9. Read Matthew 20:26 and underline it in your Bible. According to this verse, who is considered great? Are *you* able to meet that requirement for greatness? How? Be specific. Write a prayer asking God to help you serve Him and others.

10. Pray the prayer out loud on page 119. Include the specifics of your life that God has brought to mind while studying this chapter.

Read Chapter 14: "Believing It's Not Over till It's Over"

1. Have you ever feared that God has no purpose for your life, or if He did at one time He has no further use for you now? Or have you ever gone through so many changes that it seemed as though everything was falling apart rather than moving into a deeper fulfillment of God's purpose for your life? Explain your answer.

2. God sometimes has to shut off the way things have been in our lives so He can bring us into a new time. Are you ready for a new time and work of the Holy Spirit in your life or is that something you dread or fear? Explain your answer.

3. Describe the last major life change that you experienced. (For example, a move, death of a loved one, divorce, injury, loss of job, loss of a friend, etc.) Did that experience feel like the end of something? Did that experience bring about the beginning of something else? Explain.

4. Is there anything you are experiencing now, or have experienced in the recent past, that seems as though it could be the end of something? Are you able to see the possibility of a new beginning in it? If so, describe that. If not, write a prayer asking God to help you let go of the old thing that is changing and be able to embrace the new thing He is doing.

5. Read Psalm 92:13-14 and underline these verses in your Bible. What does God's Word say about our later years? _____

_____.

Great men and women of the Bible, like Noah, Moses, and Abraham, were called to do their greatest work in their later years. Why do you think God called them at that time in their lives? Do you believe that God might call you to do your greatest work in your later years for those same reasons? Explain.

6. Read Proverbs 19:20 and underline it in your Bible. In light of this verse, why is it important to be in the Word, attend church regularly, and receive counsel from godly people?

7. Read Psalm 71:18 and underline it in your Bible. Using that verse, write out a prayer for your life and your future.

8. If life as you have known it seems to be changing, and the path you have walked seems to be ending, what could that be a sign of? (See page 125, second paragraph.) What should you do at times like that? (See page 125, third paragraph.)

9. When major changes happen in your life, are you fearful and resistant or do you find it easy to trust God through them? Explain. Write a prayer telling God that you want to be open to the changes He wants to bring about in your life. If change is difficult for you, ask Him to help you learn to trust Him through those times.

10. Pray the prayer out loud on page 126. Include the specifics of your life that God has brought to mind while studying this chapter.

WEEK *Fifteen*

Read Chapter 15: "Surviving Disappointment"

1. Often our greatest times of disappointment come when _____
   _____.
   The level of fulfillment and happiness we experience in our lives doesn't depend on other people, it depends on _____. (See page 130, first paragraph.) We make a mistake in expecting too much from ourselves, _____, and _____, when our expectations should be from _____. (See page 131, first paragraph.)

2. Have you ever been greatly disappointed by someone? Write out a prayer asking God to help you forgive that person for what they did or did not do that so disappointed you.

3. Read Micah 7:8 and underline it in your Bible. What does this verse speak to you about your times of disappointment?

4. Why does God sometimes allow hard things to happen in our lives? (See page 131, last paragraph.) Can you think of an example in your life where you went through a difficult time, but God brought good out of it? Explain.

5. Read 1 Corinthians 4:5 and underline it in your Bible. Why should we try not to fall into great disappointment when things don't turn out the way we thought they would?

6. Read Psalm 138:8 and underline it in your Bible. What concerns you the most in your life right now? What does this verse speak to you about that?

7. It pleases God when you have faith enough in the midst of your disappointment to _____
_____.
(See page 132, fourth paragraph.) Write out a prayer asking God to increase your faith so that no disappointment in your life will cause you to become bitter or unforgiving.

8. When you experience disappointment what should you do? (See page 132, last paragraph.)

9. Read Psalm 16 and underline the verses that especially speak to you. Write in your own words what this section of Scripture says to you concerning going through a time of disappointment.

10. Pray the prayer out loud on page 133. Include the specifics of your life that God has brought to mind while studying this chapter.

Week *Sixteen*

Read Chapter 16: "Traveling Through the
Dark Moments of Relationships"

1. Our darkest hours can come because of the troubled
   times we have with _____. But
   much of what God wants to work in us will come
   about as we _____
   _____
   _____.
   (See page 135, first and last paragraphs.) What does
   the enemy of your soul want to see happen in your
   relationships? Why? (See page 136, first paragraph.)

2. Do you have a particular relationship that troubles you right now? Explain. How would you like to see it change? Write out a prayer releasing that person to God and praying for that change.

3. Every relationship requires a _____. Every sacrifice has a _____. What is the sacrifice we must make in a relationship? (See page 137, first paragraph.) Are you willing to make that sacrifice in your troubling relationships? Explain why or why not.

4. What sacrifice could you make today for your most important or most troubling relationship? Describe.

5. Read Philippians 2:3-4 and underline these two verses in your Bible. Write them out as a prayer over your most challenging or important relationship. (For example, "Lord, in my relationship with (person's name), I pray that nothing I do will be done through selfish ambition…" etc.)

6. What can you do to resurrect a relationship that has suffered deep wounds? _____

_____.

(See page 137, second paragraph.) Write out a prayer asking God to help you put the other person in your relationship before yourself.

7. Read Ephesians 4:31-32 and underline these verses in your Bible. Describe in your own words what you should do with regards to your relationships.

8. Read 2 Corinthians 6:14 and underline it in your Bible. Do you have a relationship with anyone who is either not a believer, or who is such a weak believer that they influence you away from a strong walk with the Lord? Explain. How could you pray about that relationship? Write out a prayer for each of your friends or family members who don't know the Lord. Ask God to bring them into a full knowledge of Him.

9. In ironing out the wrinkles in relationships, it's best
   to release and cling to _____. The stronger your
   relationship with _____, the better your other
   relationships will be. (See page 141, first paragraph.)
   Write out a prayer releasing each of your relationships to God. Be specific.

10. Pray the prayer out loud on pages 141-142. Include
    the specifics of your life that God has brought to
    mind while studying this chapter.

WEEK *Seventeen*

Read Chapter 17: "Walking in the
Midst of the Overwhelming"

1. What kinds of situations do you find most overwhelming in your life? Explain. How do you handle
   those situations? How would you like to see God
   answer your prayers about them?

2. Read Psalm 61:1-4 and underline these verses in your Bible. What does this section of Scripture speak to you about overwhelming situations? What should you do when you are in those kinds of circumstances?

3. Does being afraid necessarily mean that God is not with you, you are out of God's will, or you are a spiritual weakling? _____. What *could* fear be a sign of? (See page 147, second paragraph.)

4. What is the most overwhelming situation you are facing in your life at this time? Why do you feel overwhelmed by it? Read Psalm 77:1-9 and underline the verses that describe your experience. List those verses here.

5. Read Psalm 27:1 and underline it in your Bible. Why should you not be afraid in the midst of overwhelming circumstances?

6. Read Psalm 77:10-14 and underline these verses in your Bible. What things has God done for you in the past when you felt overwhelmed, that encourage you now when you remember them? Or what did God do for someone in the Bible, that gives you comfort when you think about it?

7. Any sign of fear should be a call to _____. The moment you feel fear, draw immediately_____ _____. Get a sense of and _____ and allow His _____ to penetrate your situation. The deeper we press into _____, the more of His _____ we experience, and the less _____ we will have. (See page 148, third and fourth paragraphs.) Write out a prayer asking God to help you remember to draw close to Him at the first recognition of fear so that His perfect love can cast it out.

8. Read 1 John 4:18 and underline it in your Bible. What takes away our fear? _____.
Who is the only one who embodies perfect love? _____. Can you think of a time when you were afraid, but as you drew close to God the fear went away? Describe.

9. Do you have fear about anything right now? Write out a prayer telling God about it. Be specific. Ask Him to show you how to pray regarding this. Then ask Him to give you a special sense of His presence, love, and peace and remove the fear.

10. Pray the prayer out loud on page 149. Include the specifics of your life that God has brought to mind while studying this chapter.

WEEK *Eighteen*

Read Chapter 18: "Reaching for
God's Hand in Times of Loss"

1. What would you say is the worst time of loss you have
   ever experienced? How would you describe your feelings at the time? Were you able to rely on God through
   it? Why or why not?

2. How did you get over your loss? Do you feel you have recovered from that loss now? Do things seem "back to normal"? Can your life ever be the same again? Explain.

3. Read Matthew 5:4 and underline it in your Bible. While the compassion, sympathy, and love of others can be a great comfort to us in our time of grief, where do we find the only healing touch that can comfort and restore us completely? (See page 153, first paragraph.) Have you experienced that kind of comfort in a time of grief? Describe.

4. Have you ever experienced someone speaking words to you in a time of loss or grief that brought you more pain? Describe. What was your reaction? Do you feel those words were intended to hurt you or were they just expressed unknowingly? Have you been able to forgive that person for their words and see the love behind them? Explain.

5. What are some things that people have done for you during times of loss or grief that you found to be especially helpful?

6. What two things should you never confuse, especially during a time of loss? What happens when you do confuse them? (See page 154, first paragraph.)

7. Read Psalm 119:49-50 and underline these two verses in your Bible. What will be a source of comfort to you in your time of grief? _____.
What else will be a source of comfort in a time of loss? (See page 155, last paragraph.) Do you feel you are able to draw close to the Lord and seek His presence in your time of loss and grief? Why or why not?

8. Have there been any experiences of loss in your life that still cause you great pain to remember? Are there certain events in your past that you cannot even bear to think about? If so, explain below and write out a prayer releasing that loss into God's hands. Ask Him to heal your heart and thank Him that there is an end to it, which you look forward to experiencing.

9. Read Isaiah 60:19-20 and underline these verses in your Bible. What does God's Word speak to you about any dark time of loss and grief you may experience? Write down the sections of this Scripture that speak most strongly to your heart and give you courage to face any dark time of loss.

10. Pray the prayer out loud on pages 155-156. Include the specifics of your life that God has brought to mind while studying this chapter.

WEEK *Nineteen*

Read Chapter 19: "Stepping out of the Past"

1. Read Isaiah 43:18-19 and underline these verses in your Bible. What does God say about your past?

2. Why do we have to step out of the past? What is the main thing that will keep us from ever being completely free of it? (See page 157, first and last paragraphs.)

3. In order to get free of unforgiveness, we have to let go of everything except _____. Why do we often refuse to extend forgiveness to others? (See page 158, third and fourth paragraphs.)

4. Read 2 Corinthians 5:17 and underline it in your Bible. What is the promise for anyone who comes to know the Lord?

5. Read 2 Corinthians 4:16 and underline it in your Bible. Even though we have become a new creation when we receive Jesus, do we need to be renewed in our soul? Where do you feel you need to be renewed in your soul today? Explain.

6. If there have been injustices committed against you in the past, does that mean you are not responsible for your attitudes now? Explain. (See page 159, last paragraph and top of page 160.)

7. Has there been anything that has happened in your past that you feel has kept you from moving into the future God has for you? Explain. Do you believe Christ can redeem your past? If so, write out a prayer asking God to set you free from these past events. If you don't feel Jesus can redeem your past, write out a prayer asking God to prove you wrong.

8. Read Proverbs 4:25-27 and underline these verses in your Bible. What should you do to keep from looking back into the past?

9. Looking back into the past, you see _____
    _____.
    Looking too far forward, you see _____
    _____.
    It's best to embrace _____ and say, "God, give
    me _____."
    (See page 161, second paragraph.) The way we step
    out of the past is to walk _____. Explain
    how we walk in the Spirit. (See page 162, first para-
    graph.)

10. Pray the prayer out loud on page 163. Include the
    specifics of your life that God has brought to mind
    while studying this chapter.

Read Chapter 20: "Maintaining a Passion for the Present"

1. Pastor Jack Hayford says, "Don't let where you are become _____
   _____."
   (See page 166, first paragraph.) Have you ever feared that where you were at the moment was an indication of where you were going to be forever? Explain.

2. Read Ephesians 5:8 and underline it in your Bible. How can you walk as a child of the light? (See page 166, second paragraph from the bottom.) Write out a prayer asking God to help you walk as a child of the light.

3. What happens when you walk with a leading from the Lord? (See page 166, last paragraph.)

4. What happens to our lives when we don't have a clear leading from God? (See page 167, second paragraph.)

5. Can you think of a time you made choices without a clear leading from the Lord? What was the result of doing that? How would you do it differently today?

6. Read Romans 8:18 and underline it in your Bible. According to this verse, why should you not worry about the difficult times you are going through?

7. What is the most challenging thing you are facing today? No matter how large or small it is, explain it below and write a prayer asking God to be in charge and either take away the situation or walk you victoriously through it.

8. Read Matthew 5:16 and underline it in your Bible. In what way can you be an extension of God's light to others today? If you are not sure, ask Him to show you and then write what He reveals to you below.

9. Read Philippians 4:6-7 and underline these verses in your Bible. Instead of being anxious about things today, what could you do instead? What will be the result?

10. Pray the prayer out loud on pages 169 and 170. Include the specifics of your life that God has brought to mind while studying this chapter.

WEEK *Twenty-One*

Read Chapter 21: "Moving into Your Future"

1. Complete the following sentences:

   We wonder if God remembers who we are, but He
   _____. We wait for God to
   notice our plight, but He waits _____.
   We see ourselves in the dark because we've done
   something wrong, but He sees us _____
   _____.
   God moves powerfully at our request, but we don't
   even _____. We have trou-
   ble trusting God with our future, but the future He
   has for us is _____. (See page
   171, second paragraph.)

2. What is your greatest concern about your future?

3. Read 1 Corinthians 2:9 and Romans 8:38-39 and underline them in your Bible. How do these verses make you feel about your concerns for the future? Explain.

4. Read Proverbs 16:9 again in your Bible. Do you think this verse means we should not make plans for the future? What does this verse say to you? (See page 172, first paragraph.)

5. Why should we not look so far ahead that we neglect to take proper steps today? (See page 172, last paragraph.)

6. What is the common thread in the experiences of Noah, Abraham, and Moses? (See page 173, last three paragraphs and first paragraph on page 174.) What lessons does their walk with God speak to you?

7. Complete the following sentences:

God is not asking me to be perfect. He is asking me to

_____.

God is not asking me to have my whole future figured out. He is asking me to _____

_____.

(See page 174, third paragraph.) Write out a prayer asking God to help you to trust Him for your future. Be specific.

8. Are we supposed to do whatever we want to do and then ask God to bless it? _____. Have you ever done that? _____. What was the result? _____
   _____.

   What are we to do instead? _____
   _____
   _____.

   (See page 173, second paragraph.) Write out a prayer asking God to show you what you are to do with regards to your future and then tell Him you want Him to lead you into it and bless it.

9. Read Jeremiah 29:11 and Isaiah 60:1-2 and underline them in your Bible. What do these verses speak to you about your future?

10. Pray the prayer out loud on pages 175-176. Include the specifics of your life that God has brought to mind while studying this chapter.

Notes

CHAPTER ONE

1. Jack Hayford, *Pursuing the Will of God* (Sisters, OR: Multnomah Publishing, 1997), p. 20.

CHAPTER THREE

1. Oswald Chambers, *My Utmost Devotional Bible* (Nashville, TN: Thomas Nelson Publishers, 1992), p. 44.

CHAPTER SIX

1. Oswald Chambers, *My Utmost Devotional Bible* (Nashville, TN: Thomas Nelson Publishers, 1992), p. 11.

CHAPTER SEVEN

1. Oswald Chambers, *My Utmost Devotional Bible* (Nashville, TN: Thomas Nelson Publishers, 1992), p. 98.

CHAPTER THIRTEEN

1. Oswald Chambers, *My Utmost Devotional Bible* (Nashville, TN: Thomas Nelson Publishers, 1992), p. 86.

CHAPTER FIFTEEN

1. Oswald Chambers, *My Utmost Devotional Bible* (Nashville, TN: Thomas Nelson Publishers, 1992), p. 86.

OTHER BOOKS by
STORMIE OMARTIAN

www.stormieomartian.com

The Power of a Praying® Wife

The Power of a Praying® Wife

The Power of a Praying® Wife
  Audio Book

The Power of a Praying® Wife
  Book of Prayers

The Power of a Praying® Wife
  Prayer & Study Guide

The Power of a Praying® Wife
  Deluxe Edition

The Power of a Praying® Woman

The Power of a Praying® Woman

The Power of a Praying® Woman *Bible*

The Power of a Praying® Woman
  Book of Prayers

The Power of a Praying® Woman
  Prayer & Study Guide

The Power of a Praying® Woman
  Deluxe Edition

The Power of a Praying® Husband

The Power of a Praying® Husband

The Power of a Praying® Husband
  Book of Prayers

The Power of a Praying® Husband
  Prayer & Study Guide

The Power of a Praying® Parent

The Power of a Praying® Parent

The Power of a Praying® Parent
  Book of Prayers

The Power of a Praying® Parent
  Prayer & Study Guide

The Power of a Praying® Parent
  Deluxe Edition

Just Enough Light for the Step I'm On

Just Enough Light for the Step I'm On

Just Enough Light for the Step I'm On...
  A Devotional Prayer Journey

Just Enough Light for the Step I'm On
  Book of Prayers

The Prayer That Changes Everything®

The Prayer That Changes Everything®

The Prayer That Changes Everything®
  Book of Prayers

The Prayer That Changes Everything®
  Prayer Cards

The Prayer That Changes Everything®
  Audio Book

The Power of Prayer to Change Your Marriage

The Power of Prayer to Change
  Your Marriage

The Power of Prayer to Change
  Your Marriage *Audio Book*

The Power of Prayer to Change
  Your Marriage *Book of Prayers*

The Power of Prayer to Change
  Your Marriage *Prayer & Study Guide*

Other Items

A Book of Prayer

Greater Health God's Way

Prayers for Emotional Wholeness

Praying Through the Bible

The Power of a Praying® Kid

The Power of a Praying® Nation

The Power of a Praying® Teen

The Power of Praying®

The Power of Praying® *Gift Collection*

The Power of Praying® Together

Stormie

Children's Books

For This Child I Prayed

What Happens When I Talk to God?

Prayers and Promises for Little Boys

Prayers and Promises for Little Girls

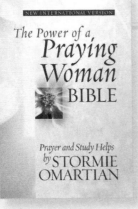

PRAY YOUR WAY THROUGH THE BIBLE, AND THE BIBLE WILL TRANSFORM YOUR PRAYERS.

Your prayer life and your Bible reading can go hand in hand with this beautiful devotional edition of the New International Version. In it Stormie Omartian provides everything you need to grow in prayer, align your prayers more closely with God's Word, and experience day by day the transforming power of the Scriptures.

- *Brief introductions* for each book of the Bible include important prayer themes.

- *Stormie's own prayers* show how to apply specific verses to your prayer life.

- *Prayer starters* lead the way as you pray for your life, your relationships, your nation, and other concerns.

- *From Stormie's Heart* pages encourage you in your daily walk with the Lord.

- *Going Deeper* articles help you interpret and apply key verses.

- *God's People at Prayer* sidebars highlight many Bible characters' experiences in prayer.

- *Prayer Is* thoughts help you keep your prayer life honest and sincere.

- *A topical reference* of all the words of Christ highlight Jesus' various teachings on forgiveness, healing, and other life-changing issues.

- *Indexes and a concordance* help you spend less time searching and more time interacting with the Scriptures.

- *Trim size*—all of these features come in a size that's perfect for your tote bag or briefcase.

Let the power of prayer and the living and active Word of God work together to help you become the person God created you to be.

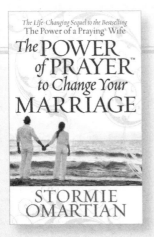

Prayer Can Change Your Marriage

It's hard to change yourself. And you can't change your spouse. But by the power of God working through your prayers, God can change you both. When you invite the Lord to rule in your marriage, He will transform both of your lives in ways you never thought possible.

Whether you are a husband or a wife, if you want your marriage to be strong and protected, this book is for you. Bestselling author Stormie Omartian addresses the deeper issues of marriage, such as

- communication breakdown, struggles with finances, and the challenge of children
- misplaced priorities, anger, unforgiveness, and finding sexual fulfillment
- infidelity, depression, negative emotions, and various destructive behaviors

No stranger to struggles in more than three decades of marriage, Stormie looks at these topics and more in the straightforward and hopeful manner millions of readers have come to trust. Included are powerful resources, such as supportive Bible verses and many personal prayers for you to pray for yourself, your spouse, and your marriage.

Your marriage can last a lifetime. Seek God in prayer, pray specifically as He leads you, and watch a miracle take place in your heart, your spouse, and your relationship.